DEVOTIONS & PRAYERS

FOR MANAGING

ANXIETY & DEPRESSION

DEVOTIONS & PRAYERS FOR MANAGING ANXIETY & DEPRESSION

COMFORT & ENCOURAGEMENT FOR TEEN BOYS

ELIJAH ADKINS

BARBOUR
PUBLISHING

Print ISBN 978-1-63609-827-2

Cover Design: Greg Jackson, Thinkpen Design

Published by Barbour Publishing, Inc., 1810 Barbour Drive, Uhrichsville, Ohio 44683, www.barbourbooks.com

Our mission is to inspire the world with the life-changing message of the Bible.

Member of the
Evangelical Christian
Publishers Association

INTRODUCTION

Do you struggle with anxiety or depression? Are you prone to crippling panic attacks, episodes of deep and inexplicable sadness, or a constant feeling that something is wrong? If so, *you're not alone.* Millions of Christian teens around the world are waging war with the twin foes of anxiety and depression. . .and many of them feel like they have nowhere to turn for help.

Well, here's some good news! This book exists to point teens like you toward the hope that's found in the pages of God's Word. The great Creator, who made you and fashioned your unique mind and personality, also understands your struggle—and He hasn't left you to fend for yourself. As you'll soon learn, our loving God has given His children many tools they can use to push back against despair.

Make no mistake: the road may get rough at times, but hopefully, this book will open your eyes to the personal God who's empowering you every step of the way.

So hang on—there's hope just around the corner!

PRIMAL FEAR

*And [Adam] said, "I heard the sound of you
in the garden, and I was afraid, because
I was naked, and I hid myself."*
GENESIS 3:10 ESV

. . . .

Today's verse marks the first time fear is mentioned in the Bible. It comes after Adam and Eve do the one thing God said they shouldn't: eat from the tree of the knowledge of good and evil. Suddenly, their blissful life is polluted by the presence of soul-staining sin, corrupted by guilt and the dread of punishment.

All anxiety from that point forward has one common source: our weakness as human beings. Though we're made in the image of God, we no longer bear His perfection and certainly not His power. We're fragile, sinful creatures, stumbling fearfully in the dark.

At least. . .that's what we *used* to be. But with God in our lives through our faith in Jesus Christ, this primal fear is nothing more than an obsolete relic of our ancestors' sin. While we're here on earth, we'll struggle with the emotions of dread and sadness, but God has stripped away all reason for their existence. No longer do we have to fear the future or the wrath of our Creator—because of His love, we're safe at last.

PRAYER STARTER:
*God, thank You for stepping into human
history to conquer fear once and for all.*

SURGING FEAR

Such love has no fear, because perfect love
expels all fear. If we are afraid, it is for fear
of punishment, and this shows that we have
not fully experienced his perfect love.
1 JOHN 4:18 NLT

. . . .

Anxiety is a terrifying beast, not the least because it often comes without warning, surging to devastating heights before we even see it coming. Worse yet, one of the strongest fears that torments God's children can come in the form of fearing God Himself.

Because we can't see God or speak with Him face-to-face, it's tempting to jump to conclusions about His attitude toward us. And once our anxious minds have convinced us that God is angry, it's nearly impossible to rationalize these emotions away.

That's why daily Bible reading is so important. Verses like today's let us know exactly how God feels about His children. Once we grasp God's perfect love toward us, we'll realize that there's no need to listen to our anxiety—it's just an emotion. So, when the waves of worry come, we can ride them out, resting safely in the comfort of God's love.

PRAYER STARTER:

God, thank You for giving me a solid truth I can grasp when anxiety knocks me off my feet. No matter how fiercely fear swells in my mind, Your love will help me overcome it.

THE DARKEST VALLEY

*Even when I walk through the darkest valley, I will
not be afraid, for you are close beside me. Your
rod and your staff protect and comfort me.*
PSALM 23:4 NLT

. . . .

The beginning of today's verse sounds like the setting
for a horror film. It conjures images of a deep, dark
ravine in the wilderness, surrounded by evil forces
that are felt but never seen.

Perhaps this imagery sounds all too real to you. If
you've ever suffered from anxiety or depression, you
know what this "darkest valley" is—a sleepless, tormented night. . .the crushing weight of loneliness. . .the
fear that all is lost. . .the pain of uncertainty.

The psalmist knew this fear, but he also knew a
love that is stronger than fear. He knew that no matter
what his mind screamed, God was right by his side. He
knew that in his life of shadows, God was illuminating
his path. And he knew that no matter how dangerous
the path appeared, the Lord was steadying his steps.

How wonderful it is to know that God's light shines
even in the darkest valley!

PRAYER STARTER:

*Lord, take my hand when I feel overwhelmed.
Let me feel Your presence in the valley of fear.*

A STEADY NOTE

Let the peace of Christ have power over your hearts. You were chosen as a part of His body. Always be thankful.
COLOSSIANS 3:15 NLV

. . . .

At first glance, today's verse sounds like one of those shallow, bumper-sticker sayings. After all, how can an anxious teen have peace during a panic attack? It's difficult to count your blessings when it feels like your world is ending.

But the end of the scripture passage holds the key: "*Always* be thankful." Gratitude isn't some secret weapon you pull out in the fog of battle; it's a way of life—a gradual reworking of your brain into a Christlike mindset. So, even when you aren't feeling anxious, practice being thankful. Think of the good things God has done for you—starting with salvation and moving on to all the little joys that fill your life.

Slowly, this attitude of thanksgiving will become your go-to reaction to every minor setback. Even if it doesn't entirely remove your anxiety, it will serve as a steady note to ground you in a sea of deafening, angry noise—a peace in the middle of the storm.

PRAYER STARTER:

Father, thank You for all the ways You've blessed me. Remind me of these blessings when it feels like everything has been taken away.

SUPERCOMPUTER

*Trust in the Lord with all your heart, and do
not trust in your own understanding.*
PROVERBS 3:5 NLV

. . . .

God has gifted each of us with an amazing machine—a
supercomputer that's capable of solving complex problems at a moment's notice. It's always scanning its
surroundings, searching for the best possible route.

If you haven't guessed by now, this machine is
your brain—one of God's most astounding creations.
But just like everything else in this fallen world, your
brain isn't immune to glitches and system failures.
Sometimes, when faced with an exceptionally hard
problem, your brain will kick into overdrive, cycling
through millions of possibilities and overheating in
the process. The only way to stop this cycle of pain?
To step back, admit your lack of understanding, and
leave things in God's hands.

Of course, this isn't always easy—your brain will
try its best to pick the problem back up again. But don't
let it! Each time the cycle begins, stand strong and
refuse to repeat the process. It may take weeks or even
months, but eventually, you'll discover the freedom of
leaning on God's understanding instead of your own.

PRAYER STARTER:

*Lord, a thousand questions are eating away at
me. But today, I'm ending the search for answers,
trusting that You already hold the solution.*

A GOOD WORD

Anxiety in a person's heart weighs it down,
but a good word makes it glad.
PROVERBS 12:25 NASB

. . . .

Think of the last time you waited nervously for something. Maybe it was for the grade on a final exam, the outcome to an important conversation, or a "yes" or "no" to an application you'd submitted. Over the course of the next few hours or days, your palms got sweaty and your face flushed as uncertainty poked cruelly at your mind. Suddenly, just when it seemed you couldn't take it anymore, the answer finally came. . .and it was good news!

That's the kind of anxiety today's verse addresses. Sometimes, it takes the form of a general sense of unease—the fear that something is wrong or that bad news is just around the bend. But you don't have to let this fear spiral out of control. Instead, you can open your Bible, where you're certain to find a "good word" to lift your spirits. No matter how a particular situation turns out, God's eternal promises will always hold true for His children. We don't have to wait in fear—we *know* God always wins.

PRAYER STARTER:

Father, thank You for giving me a reason to
relax. No matter what happens, Your promises
will always be enough to make me glad.

BIG BAG OF WORRIES

*"Come to Me, all who are weary and
burdened, and I will give you rest."*
MATTHEW 11:28 NASB

. . . .

In *The Pilgrim's Progress* by John Bunyan, the main character, Christian, carries a massive load on his shoulders, symbolizing the sin and guilt that weighs heavily on his soul. But when he approaches the cross, this load miraculously falls from his back, tumbling into an empty tomb. At last, he is free.

As Christians, we've left our load of sin at the cross. . .but how often do we pick up smaller loads along the way? How often do we think that even though God removed our guilt, He somehow can't take away our worry?

Maybe your burden lies in peer pressure, loneliness, fear of the future, or simply a generalized anxiety about life. No matter what it is, Jesus is calling you to carry it to Him. He's standing with open arms, ready to remove the load that weighs you down and carry it to a place where it'll never be seen again. There's no need to haul around the weight of the world, especially when you belong to the one who holds it in the palm of His hand!

PRAYER STARTER:

*Take my burden of fear, doubt, depression,
and pain, God. Only You can free my soul.*

UNEARTHLY PEACE

Peace I leave with you, my peace I give unto you:
not as the world giveth, give I unto you. Let not
your heart be troubled, neither let it be afraid.
JOHN 14:27 KJV

. . . .

Is it possible to have peace while you're dealing with anxiety and depression? Is it possible to feel like everything is caving in. . .while at the same time fully trusting God is holding your life together?

Today's verse says *yes.*

Even as fear snarls and snaps, Jesus promises to give you a calm that curbs your emotions. Even when hopelessness sets in and you're tempted to give in to despair, He promises to anchor your soul to an everlasting hope. Even in the pain, peace is within reach.

By reflecting on God's character and Jesus' sacrifice so you could be saved, you can still the storm in your mind and rest in the peace that God has planted in your heart. Soon, these attacks will begin losing their power, and your attitude of peace will become second nature.

The world can't offer this hope—it's an unexplainable peace that comes straight from the love of God Himself.

PRAYER STARTER:

Lord, my goal is to focus on Your power and love
instead of the intensity of my problems. Teach
me to always rest in Your perfect peace.

SELF-SABOTAGE

"For this reason I say to you, do not be worried about your life, as to what you will eat or what you will drink. . . . Which of you by worrying can add a single day to his life's span?"
MATTHEW 6:25, 27 NASB

. . . .

As with most things in life, worry has a time and a place. That speech you're about to give in class? A small amount of worry can give you the motivation you need to practice. That test coming up tomorrow? If you didn't feel a little bit nervous, it probably means you don't care.

But that's not the kind of worry Jesus spoke of in today's verses. When worry gets out of hand—when we start fretting over things we can't control—it's time to step back and learn just how pointless this worry is. Worry doesn't help anything; it's more connected to self-sabotage than survival.

So, when you find yourself losing sleep over what tomorrow might bring, remember that the only one who knows the future is God. . .and He's got everything worked out (Romans 8:28).

PRAYER STARTER:

Lord, I know You have my best interests in mind, so I'm turning over my future to You. No more worrying—I'm willing to go wherever You take me.

ALL THINGS

*I can do all things through Christ
which strengtheneth me.*
PHILIPPIANS 4:13 KJV

. . . .

Many people have tried to twist today's verse to suit their own wants. *I can do all things*, they think, *so I guess that means I can rule the world!*

Nice try, but not quite. In context, this verse is Paul's way of saying that no matter how many trials come his way, he can withstand it all with God's help. Naturally, you can apply this truth to any problem you encounter—physical or mental. That's what "all things" means.

Are you struggling with deep depression and don't know if you'll make it through to tomorrow? You can do *all things* through Christ. Are you in the middle of a panic attack, feeling utterly helpless as your own mind assaults you? You can do *all things* through Christ. Are you caught somewhere in between, searching for purpose amid life's monotony? You can do *all things* through Christ.

Whatever your struggle, Jesus is right there, offering strength when you need it the most. Are you reaching for Him today?

PRAYER STARTER:

*Through You, Jesus, I can withstand anything.
I'm not cowering in fear any longer—I know
You've conquered it once and for all.*

FEAR-ERASING LOVE

When I am afraid, I will put my trust in You.
PSALM 56:3 NASB

. . . .

A lot of Christians treat fear like it's a sin—like it's something you only feel when you're disobeying God. But as anyone suffering anxiety knows, this just isn't true. In fact, this kind of thinking usually makes anxiety even worse.

While the Bible does tell us not to fear, God also knows that fear is sometimes a natural response—like blinking when something is thrown toward your face. And when the brain itself is misfiring, fear can mushroom into monstrous proportions. That's why today's verse says, "*When* I am afraid." The psalmist realizes fear *will* come. . .but he also knows a way he can fight it.

God knows it's impossible to completely avoid fear, but He doesn't want us to stay stuck in it. Instead, He's told us about Himself to comfort us in our struggle. When we don't know why something is happening—sickness or pain or death—we can trust that God does, giving us a reason to put fear behind us.

Where are you putting your trust?

PRAYER STARTER:

Almighty God, thank You for Your fear-erasing love. Teach me how to conquer the part of me that worries, so I can freely serve You.

A GLIMMER OF HOPE

Now faith is being sure we will get what we hope for. It is being sure of what we cannot see.

HEBREWS 11:1 NLV

. . . .

If you had to pinpoint a single cause of depression and anxiety, what would it be? Most likely, it would look something like a blend of hopelessness and uncertainty. You don't know how the future will play out—you just know it's going to be bad.

Now it's time for a fresh perspective. If this dreadful brand of pessimism is fueling your fear and sadness, then what's the *opposite* of that?

It's faith! Without faith, your life will have no meaning or direction. You'll be stumbling through the dark, fearfully waiting for that one misstep to plunge you into the pit. But if you have faith in God, the creator of reality and the lover of your soul, then what need is there for fear or gloominess? You have the single greatest gift in the universe and a personal relationship with the one who gave it. You may not know what this life will bring, but you know what lies at its end—the shining, eternal light of peace.

PRAYER STARTER:

Thank You, Jesus, for giving me a hope to cling to when it appears there's no reason to keep going. Thank You for faith.

ON EAGLES' WINGS

*But they that wait upon the LORD shall renew
their strength; they shall mount up with
wings as eagles; they shall run, and not be
weary; and they shall walk, and not faint.*
ISAIAH 40:31 KJV

. . . .

Time and again, the Bible proves the old proverb: what doesn't kill you makes you stronger. Moses dropped his doubt and followed God, becoming the greatest leader Israel ever had. David was hunted by innumerable foes, but his brushes with death only strengthened his faith. Three Hebrew men passed, quite literally, through the fiery furnace, emerging alive and well with a song of praise on their lips.

Anxiety and depression are no different. They're just blustering winds, trying their best to pull you down. . .all while God uses them to lift you above the clouds to see the glory of the sun. Your fear—of pain, of being alone, of what the future holds—isn't the end; it's merely a means through which God is growing you into the man He's destined you to become.

So today, stop trying to hide from the emotions that surge within you; instead, praise God for using them to lift you up into the life He's called you to live.

PRAYER STARTER:

*God, help me learn from my struggles,
not give in to them. When Satan tries
to pull me down, teach me to rise.*

THROUGH ENEMY LINES

For the angel of the LORD is a guard;
he surrounds and defends all who fear him.
PSALM 34:7 NLT

. . . .

Imagine what it would be like to be surrounded by bodyguards. Even while walking through a crowd of potential enemies, you'd feel little to no fear. The moment someone steps out to do you harm, muscular guys would slam him to the ground like pro football players. And, as the crowd watches, the bodyguards would haul away your battered, would-be assailant—for good.

Well, that's exactly what it's like to be a child of God. Once you place your faith in Him, you're protected by a guardian angel. This angel works to keep you from physical harm, but he's even more concerned about your spiritual well-being. So even when it feels like you're surrounded by evil, don't be afraid: God's got you covered. The devil can talk all he likes, but he knows the moment he tries to lift a finger against you, he'll face the full wrath of God's elite.

Today, don't listen to Satan's lies. As long as God is by your side, you're as safe as safe can be.

PRAYER STARTER:

Thank You, Father, for watching over me
when I'm frightened. Give me courage as
I walk by faith through enemy lines.

TOXIC THOUGHTS

Whatever is true, whatever is honorable, whatever is right, whatever is pure, whatever is lovely, whatever is commendable. . .think about these things.
PHILIPPIANS 4:8 NASB

. . . .

Sometimes, anxiety and depression come without warning, striking the brain like a plague and not letting go until help is sought and given.

Other times, however, these negative emotions can largely be traced back to a single source: your thought life. If you surround yourself with negative messages—whether they're from social media, your friends at school, or even the nightly news—then sooner or later, you'll start internalizing these ideas.

Of course, there's no way to completely avoid negativity in this life. But we can make time each day for a "detox"—a scheduled time dedicated to removing ourselves from the world's distractions and focusing on nothing but prayer and God's Word. Without these life-saving periods of spiritual rest, our souls will become increasingly stained and corrupted, resulting in feelings of fear and despair. But when your focus shifts to the things described in today's verse, a healing salve is placed on your mind, reshaping it into the image of Christ.

PRAYER STARTER:

Lord, teach me to dwell on Your truth.

BACKSEAT DRIVER

*Be quiet and know that I am God. I will be honored
among the nations. I will be honored in the earth.*
PSALM 46:10 NLV

. . . .

Have you ever met a "backseat driver"—someone who,
no matter the situation, is always worrying about how
another person should complete a task? If so, you
probably know how annoying it is. . .especially when
this "advice" lies outside the person's area of expertise.

Well, the truth is we can sometimes act like backseat drivers to God. Every time He makes an unexpected
turn, we lean forward, pushing against our restraints,
and shout, "No! Keep going straight! Watch out for
the pothole! Don't hit that car! You're going too fast!"
Pretty soon, we've got ourselves so worked up that
when God turns around and says, "Be quiet," it's not out
of exasperation but out of concern for our well-being.

God *always* knows what He's doing—He doesn't
need our startled cries or complaints to guide Him
along. The only way we can find peace is by leaning
back and accepting wherever He goes, knowing that He
is God and that He will always be honored in the earth.

PRAYER STARTER:

*Lord, help me be a willing passenger in Your
plan, not a backseat driver. Give me the faith to
know You're leading me to the best outcome.*

JESUS IN THE BOAT

*And He got up and rebuked the wind and said to
the sea, "Hush, be still." And the wind died down
and it became perfectly calm. And He said to them,
"Why are you afraid? Do you still have no faith?"*
MARK 4:39–40 NASB

Today's passage proves just how strong Jesus is. When confronted with a raging hurricane, Jesus didn't take time to gather His power or prepare for a struggle with the wind. No, He simply awoke from His sleep and said, perhaps with a yawn, "Hush, be still." And just like that, the storm vanished.

When we're in the midst of a tumultuous bout of anxiety, it can be easy to forget Jesus' power—just as the disciples did when they saw the wind and rain. The urgency of the moment drowns out our knowledge of God's infinite capabilities, like a raging flood in our soul. But know this: Jesus can calm a storm anytime He wants. So, if you're still suffering, it's all somehow part of His plan.

Knowing that Jesus is with us in our boat can provide an immeasurable sense of peace, even as the storms of anxiety rage on. Who's in your boat today?

PRAYER STARTER:

*Lord, I know You can calm this storm. Please grant
me the faith to see Your power instead of the wind's.*

NO MORE A SLAVE

For ye have not received the spirit of bondage again to fear; but ye have received the Spirit of adoption, whereby we cry, Abba, Father.
ROMANS 8:15 KJV

. . . .

If you've ever struggled with anxiety and depression, you know how fitting this verse's metaphor is. Despair is like a cruel slave owner, pushing you to work harder and harder. . .yet only layering on punishment the harder you try.

That's not the life God has called you to live. Instead of enslaving you, God has adopted you into His family. Your identity lies not in your darkest fears but rather in the shining future that awaits you on the other side, in eternity. Fear and sorrow can crack their whips all they want, but you can turn the tables by standing up and introducing them to your new Father. Faced with such glory and truth, the forces of evil will eventually have no choice but to cower and hide, dropping their instruments of torment along the way.

You may have been a slave once, but those days are over. Now, you're a child of the King.

PRAYER STARTER:

Almighty Father, I'm so glad to be a part of Your family. With You by my side, anxiety and depression don't stand a chance!

THE BEST MEDICINE

A merry heart doeth good like a medicine:
but a broken spirit drieth the bones.
PROVERBS 17:22 KJV

. . . .

The opinions of doctors are finally catching up to the truth of the Bible: laughter really is the best medicine. Not only can it improve your immune system and relieve tension, it can actually do wonders for your mental health. According to one study, it helps to take whatever is bothering you—whatever disappointment or stressful situation you're facing—and reframe it in a humorous light. Purposefully seek out relatable humor, learning to laugh at the things that might normally drag you down.

You're a child of God, and no amount of hardship or stress can rip you from His care. So why not make the most of the life He's given you? Embrace His blessings, and don't take the endless trivial concerns so seriously. The devil loves to see you stress over all the things you can't control, so the best way to thwart his attempts is to laugh in his face.

Depression is no laughing matter. . .but laughter is always a great place to start the healing.

PRAYER STARTER:

Lord God, remind me to laugh when I feel down.
Show me how to care about the things that
matter. . .and disregard the things that don't.

LIFELINE

But God, who comforts the discouraged,
comforted us by the arrival of Titus.
2 CORINTHIANS 7:6 NASB

When we think of the ways God comforts His followers, we usually think of a voice that speaks to us in the silence or a strange, unexplainable sense of peace that washes over us when all hope seems lost. And while He certainly does use those methods, He often uses more subtle means to comfort us.

That's why Paul, in today's verse, viewed Titus' arrival as a godsend. Surrounded by trials and persecutions (7:5), Paul needed a solid friend to pick him up and give him the encouragement he needed, so God sent one his way.

Do you have someone who's always there for you—a person who always seems to have the right words to say whenever life turns upside down? Maybe it's a parent or grandparent, or perhaps it's a friend at school or church. Either way, never dismiss this person's company as unnecessary. God may be throwing you a lifeline, a companion to help you through your darkest days.

PRAYER STARTER:

Lord, open my eyes to fellow Christians who
want to help me in my journey. Teach me how
to walk by their side, giving and receiving
encouragement as we walk toward You.

EMPTY PROMISES

These things I have spoken unto you, that
in me ye might have peace. In the world
ye shall have tribulation: but be of good
cheer; I have overcome the world.
JOHN 16:33 KJV

. . . .

Nobody ever said the Christian life would be easy.

Okay, maybe that's not entirely true. After all, a bunch of televangelists and preachers have built their entire careers around the false message of the "easy" Christian life. Yet while it may be tempting to listen to those voices, we must understand that this thinking only brings pain, because it contradicts the reality that Jesus taught. Putting our faith in such empty promises can wreck our faith in God.

But by dwelling on today's verse—by acknowledging Jesus' promise to give us peace in the middle of the storm—we can have a more realistic (and far more fulfilling) expectation of our Christian life. By focusing less on making our problems disappear and more on the one who makes them all worthwhile, we will never lose sight of our eternal goal.

PRAYER STARTER:

Lord, I'm not asking that You spare me from
all pain—I know that wouldn't be best for
me. So please walk with me when life gets
hard and teach me how to endure.

DISJOINTED CRIES

And the Holy Spirit helps us in our weakness.
For example, we don't know what God wants us
to pray for. But the Holy Spirit prays for us with
groanings that cannot be expressed in words.
ROMANS 8:26 NLT

Have you ever been so hurt—so racked by the stress of anxious thoughts and panic attacks—that you forget how to pray?

Maybe you're usually able to keep it together, going to God with a clear request. But other times, all you can do is cry and groan, rocking back and forth as your mind carries you into pits of fear. It's an awful feeling, not being able to communicate properly with the only one who can help.

But God still understands.

Because God knows our hearts, words are not always necessary. Sometimes, a broken sob is a more powerful prayer than the most eloquent speech given from the pulpit. Our cries prove our raw devotion. . .our frailty. . .our weak but unfailing determination to reach our Creator.

When you find yourself beyond words, that's where God grabs your hand and takes you all the way to His throne.

PRAYER STARTER:

Lord, whenever I'm at a loss for words,
I know You can read what's in my heart. Thank
You for listening to my disjointed cries.

BLACK HOLE

Then I will go to the altar of God, the God of my joy. And I will praise You with the harp, O God, my God. Why are you sad, O my soul? Why have you become troubled within me? Hope in God, for I will praise Him again, my help and my God.
PSALM 43:4–5 NLV

It's sort of a cliché by now, but it's still true: anxiety and depression are like black holes. Not only do they wipe out the light from your surroundings, turning everything into a sea of blackness and gloom, they are monstrous, self-feeding machines. The more depressed and anxious you become, the more power these emotions gain. Your soul becomes an unbearable center of gravity, crushing itself under its own increasing weight.

So, what can break this inherently selfish cycle? Praise!

Praise is a way to push back against the dark tides of negativity, reversing their flow. When you focus on the greatness of God, your own flaws and inabilities and failures will shrink and shrivel until their power is gone. Eventually, this black hole will become a spring of gratitude, pouring out instead of sucking in.

Are you ready to start praising God today?

PRAYER STARTER:

Lord, thank You so much for all You are. You're holy and more than capable of lighting up my life.

MAKING A DIFFERENCE

Light shines in the darkness for the godly.
They are generous, compassionate, and righteous.
PSALM 112:4 NLT

. . . .

Today's verse reminds us that even in our darkest moment, we're never cut off from God's holy light. Why? Because we can always allow His attributes to shine in our lives.

When we're depressed, there's nothing we want less than to go out and make a difference in the world. Our minds tell us to stay at home, curled up in bed, surrounded by our own four walls. But make no mistake: going out and making a difference is one thing we *must* do to break the cycle of sadness. When we turn our attention away from ourselves and toward those who need our help, God's light illuminates our lives, shining not only upon us but upon the ones we help. We become double-sided mirrors, piercing the darkness in two directions at once.

God understands that sadness is often a necessary pit stop. . .but it's never your destination. Today, rather than sink more deeply into a place you don't want to be, make every effort to climb out by serving others. Who knows? Your act of kindness may be what it takes to help someone else climb out too.

PRAYER STARTER:

God, please show me ways to break my
depression by shining Your love onto others.

BROKENHEARTED

*The LORD is near to the brokenhearted and
saves those who are crushed in spirit.*

PSALM 34:18 NASB

. . . .

When Jesus walked the earth, whom did He spend the most time with? The people who had it all together? The intelligent religious leaders of the day? The rich? The healthy? The famous and content?

No. Jesus spent most of His time with the outcasts of society—the people who'd been kicked to the curb and left to fend for themselves in a world that wanted to see them fail. He comforted the hurting, healed the diseased, and taught the unlearned. He didn't come to point out their problems—He came to be their solution (John 3:17).

So, if you feel brokenhearted—if your life feels like it's coming apart at the seams, spilling all your deepest longings into the void—let today's verse be your song. When loved ones become ill and pass away, when relationships fail, when the voices in your head grow louder than you can bear, remember that Jesus is near. In fact, the more broken and crushed your spirit feels, the closer He stands, waiting for you to reach out to Him.

PRAYER STARTER:

*Lord Jesus, be near me. I know You take
delight in comforting those who hurt,
so please do that for me today.*

WATERY PRAYERS

"Water encompassed me to the point of death.
The deep flowed around me, seaweed was
wrapped around my head. I descended to the
base of the mountains. The earth with its bars
was around me forever, but You have brought
up my life from the pit, LORD my God."
JONAH 2:5–6 NASB

. . . .

Chances are you've never prayed to God from the belly of a whale like Jonah did. You've probably never found yourself under the sea, suffocated by the water pressure and wrapped in slimy weeds.

But chances are you've felt the same emotions Jonah felt. You know what it's like to suffocate and nearly drown in an ocean of your own thoughts. You know what it's like to feel the slippery weeds of doubt and despair wrap around your mind, invading your dreams and threatening your sanity. This dreadful ocean is common to us all.

But that makes Jonah's prayer—his gratitude toward God for the deliverance he knew was coming— all the more inspiring. In your darkest hour, you too can pray, knowing your Father is still with you—even in the belly of the whale.

PRAYER STARTER:

Thank You, God, for bringing me out of this
pit. Even in my pain, I'll praise You for the
deliverance that I know lies ahead.

CONFORMING CONFINES

And be not conformed to this world: but be ye transformed by the renewing of your mind, that ye may prove what is that good, and acceptable, and perfect, will of God.
ROMANS 12:2 KJV

It's no secret: there's a mental health crisis among young people today. And while the cause varies wildly from person to person, it's not a stretch to connect this crisis to another crisis that's happening simultaneously: young people are leaving the church in droves.

Maybe you've watched other teens walk away from God to pursue a life of personal satisfaction. Maybe you've even felt the pull yourself. But no matter how strongly the world tempts us, we must remember that it promises nothing more than a life of meaninglessness and despair. What first looks like freedom soon becomes a cage of its own as we strive to adjust our minds from the perfect, unchanging will of God to the ever-shifting whims of a fallen world bent on self-destruction.

Today, listen only for God's voice—the one power that goes beyond temporary satisfaction and offers eternal purpose.

PRAYER STARTER:

Thank You, Jesus, for offering a life of meaning and true joy. Help me to hear Your voice.

PERFECT PLANS

*"For I know the plans I have for you," says the
LORD. "They are plans for good and not for
disaster, to give you a future and a hope."*
JEREMIAH 29:11 NLT

. . . .

As Christians, we know that God is in control. But how many of us *live* like He is?

When we find ourselves in a stressful situation, it's human nature to be afraid. Without this survival instinct, humans probably wouldn't last very long. The problem comes when this helpful instinct goes into overdrive—tormenting us with "what ifs" that we have no power to control. Being trapped by our circumstances is bad enough. . .but being trapped by our minds is even worse. During these moments, it's easy to forget that our future lies in the hands of someone who wants only the best for us.

Today, ask God to remind you of His plans for you. Ask Him for the faith to see His grace at work, even in the most painful circumstances. By understanding God's plans for you—not just in your mind but deep within your heart—you'll be one step closer to learning how to combat the wild emotions swirling in your brain.

PRAYER STARTER:

*Lord God, thank You for always having the best
plans for my life. Please remind me of Your
plans whenever my own plans fall through.*

"FOMO"

The Lord is my Shepherd.
I will have everything I need.
PSALM 23:1 NLV

. . . .

FOMO—the fear of missing out. If you had to name one of the most common causes of stress today, especially in young people, this would be it. Your social media feed is designed to cultivate FOMO. Advertisers prey on our FOMO. Popular television shows, celebrities, movies, and performers have built their empires on their audience's FOMO. Even that toxic friend group at your school thrives on FOMO.

FOMO drives our culture. FOMO is big business. FOMO is. . .one of the worst things to come out of modern civilization.

For a child of God, FOMO is not only absurd but outright harmful. Because the Lord is our Shepherd— our sole source of meaning in an increasingly meaningless world—why would we ever fear that we're missing out on something?

Today, make the choice to reject FOMO wherever you see it. You possess a gift that will outlast all modern trends. Even after the latest TikTok fad is nothing more than a distant memory, your relationship with God will be more relevant than ever.

PRAYER STARTER:

Help me find my purpose entirely in You, God.
I'm Your child—what more could I want?

DISTRESS

Therefore I delight in weaknesses, in insults, in distresses, in persecutions, in difficulties, in behalf of Christ; for when I am weak, then I am strong.
2 CORINTHIANS 12:10 NASB

When we think of the apostle Paul, we often see him as a sort of Christian Superman, pushing effortlessly against the forces of evil, unfazed by the countless assaults leveled at him by the world.

But today's verse hints at a far different reality. Notice that in addition to a slew of external forces that Paul said only made him stronger, there's also an *internal* force on the list: distresses. Paul was bothered by his situations: he became worried, fearful, and distressed, just like we do. There's no doubt that while he sang in the prison, awaiting his execution (Acts 16:25), Paul felt at least a small twinge of fear. In fact, even Jesus felt emotionally devastated by the death He knew would await Him on the cross (Luke 22:44).

If you are a Christian, you will experience anxiety at some point. But in moments of weakness and loss, that's when you'll find true spiritual strength to carry on.

PRAYER STARTER:

Father, lead me safely through the maze of anxiety. Help me deal honestly with my feelings. . .and eventually overcome them with the hope You offer.

THORN IN THE FLESH

*There was given to me a thorn in the flesh, a
messenger of Satan to torment me—to keep me
from exalting myself! Concerning this I pleaded
with the Lord three times that it might leave me.
And He has said to me, "My grace is sufficient
for you, for power is perfected in weakness."*

2 Corinthians 12:7–9 nasb

. . . .

Despite the best efforts of Bible scholars throughout
history, nobody has been able to discover exactly what
Paul's "thorn in the flesh" was. Was it a temptation? A
spiritual weakness? A physical defect? We'll probably
never know.

But in a way, this ambiguity is helpful for us today.
Why? Because we *all* suffer from a thorn in the flesh.
Paul's lack of specificity makes this passage universally
applicable to whatever weakness we may face—be it
anxiety, depression, or an inability to tackle life's challenge with the courage we think we should possess.

When you're at your weakest moment, hurtling
along on some unrelenting train of thought, that's when
God's strength can shine through you. By helping you
endure these awful moments, God builds your character, transforming you into the mighty warrior you
were always meant to become.

PRAYER STARTER:

Father, help me find Your strength in the pain.

YOUR OWN WORST ENEMY

*When they came to the crowd, a man came up
to Jesus. . .saying, "Lord, have mercy on my son,
because he has seizures and suffers terribly; for he
often falls into the fire and often into the water."
. . . And Jesus rebuked [the demon], and the demon
came out of him, and the boy was healed at once.*
MATTHEW 17:14–15, 18 NASB

Have you ever felt like the son in today's verses? Like
you've been seized by a force outside your control?
Trapped in your mind with the whispers of doubt,
panic, and fear? If so, you're not alone. One of the most
frightening things about anxiety is that it often feels
like you're no longer in control of yourself.

But take heart. As today's scripture proves, Jesus
has power over all demons—whether they're the literal
devils who stalk the earth or the psychological kind
that roam your mind. Jesus is in control, and He won't
let the enemy get the best of you. No matter how dark
your thoughts become, let Jesus be the Light who guides
you through to freedom.

PRAYER STARTER:

*Save me, Lord! It feels like I'm my
own worst enemy. . .but You have the
power to free me from myself.*

LEAN ON ME

For if they fall, the one will lift up his fellow:
but woe to him that is alone when he falleth;
for he hath not another to help him up.
ECCLESIASTES 4:10 KJV

. . . .

Social distancing. It's not just a pandemic response—for many teens, it's become a way of life. The luxuries of modern society—wireless earbuds, online streaming, and social media—have all painfully backfired. Instead of using these as tools to enhance the human experience, teens often use these things to isolate themselves from their peers. After all, who needs a real, face-to-face friend when you can have a thousand "friends" online?

The answer: *all* of us.

God has given us the gift of friendship so that we can lift each other up. And if that support is taken away, where does that leave us if not on the floor, unable to rise beneath the weight of our sorrow?

Today, look for people whom God might be sending your way—other Christian teens who have a heart for God and His plan. You don't have to go it alone in this life; a helping hand or a listening ear is just around the corner.

PRAYER STARTER:

Father, open my eyes to helpful friendships.
When I can't stand, teach me to lean on
the friends You've sent my way.

HARD BATTLES

Be strong and of a good courage;
be not afraid, neither be thou dismayed:
for the LORD thy God is with thee.
JOSHUA 1:9 KJV

. . . .

When you've been accustomed to feeling defeated by your own thoughts for so long, the idea of fighting back can seem overwhelming. How can you possibly overcome such a formidable foe?

Joshua must have wondered the same thing as he stepped up to take Moses' place and fight the Canaanites. While he knew God could simply destroy these enemies once and for all, Joshua also realized that God wanted him to put forth the effort and obey the command to fight. Victory wouldn't come easily, and the battles would be long—but God promised that He would be by Joshua's side, ensuring his success everywhere he went.

Today, don't settle for a life of fear and sadness. Don't be ashamed to seek help—to use your entire arsenal of depression-fighting tools that God has mercifully provided His children. Stand up and wage war against despair itself, trusting that God will provide the victory.

PRAYER STARTER:

Lord, thank You for giving me multiple avenues
to work through my anxiety and depression.

FOOLISH WISDOM

Do not be wise in your own eyes. Fear the Lord and turn away from what is sinful. It will be healing to your body and medicine to your bones.
PROVERBS 3:7–8 NLV

. . . .

A surefire way to sign up for a lifetime of worry and stress is trying to convince yourself and others that you have everything figured out. Soon, your self-confidence will implode as it becomes apparent how much you really *don't* know. But rather than admit your error, you exhaust yourself in a never-ending quest to justify your mistakes.

Sounds terrible, doesn't it? Sadly, all too many people live like this—and not only teenagers, but many adults too. Being "wise in your own eyes" is just code for being a fool. So instead of trying to figure everything out on your own, attempting to carry the world on shoulders that were never meant to bear such burdens, give all your unanswered questions to God. He has the answers. . .and He can be trusted.

PRAYER STARTER:

All-knowing God, thank You for always having the answers. Today, I'm letting go and giving all my problems to You.

A BETTER PLACE

He maketh me to lie down in green pastures:
he leadeth me beside the still waters.
PSALM 23:2 KJV

. . . .

Doesn't today's verse sound wonderful? As you trudge through a wasteland of depressing, tormenting thoughts, there's nothing more inviting than the prospect of lying in a peaceful meadow by a babbling stream. And that's exactly where God wants to lead you today.

Severe anxiety and depression are rarely treated with a prescription of "cheering up." It often takes an outside force to pull us from the darkness. Today's verse shows that God can be that outside force. The truths in His Word are like sprawling, grassy knolls, inviting weary travelers to lie down and rest. And God, our good shepherd, is willing to lead us to these peaceful fields if we'll let Him. His promises can be our refuge from the world's hostile terrain—the one place where we can recharge our spiritual energy to face another day.

If you're tired of traveling the dark, rocky roads of fear and despair, let the good shepherd guide you to a better place.

PRAYER STARTER:

Thank You, God, for offering opportunities
for rest from my anxiety and sadness. Lead
me to Your peaceful pastures today.

41

THE COURAGE TO ASK

*Beloved, I pray that in all respects you may prosper
and be in good health, just as your soul prospers.*

3 JOHN 2 NASB

. . . .

In today's verse, John comforted his readers by letting
them know he cared—that each time he knelt before
God in prayer, their names were on his lips. How reassuring it must have been for this church to know the
apostle John was praying for them!

Is there anyone in your life—at your school, church,
or home—who can offer meaningful prayers on your
behalf? When you're struggling with fear or hopelessness, do you know someone who's strong in the faith—
someone you trust to take your situation before God?

If so, talk to that person today, adding this indi-
vidual's prayers to your own. Be open and honest
about your struggles, making it clear just how much
you need God to act in your life. Prayer, after all, isn't
just a nice formality—it's a direct line to the only one
who can make a difference.

Don't you want that line to be opened today?

PRAYER STARTER:

*Lord, thank You for the countless other
Christians in Your church who are willing to
pray for their spiritual family. Give me the
courage to ask for prayer whenever I can.*

PEOPLE PLEASER

*Obviously, I'm not trying to win the approval
of people, but of God. If pleasing people were
my goal, I would not be Christ's servant.*

GALATIANS 1:10 NLT

As a teen, you probably feel pressured to "fit in" each day. While other guys your age are bullying, gossiping, and telling dirty jokes, you may feel left out, pushed to the side because of your personal convictions. Naturally, this can lead to feelings of isolation, especially when your closest friends start distancing themselves from you because of your views.

So, what's the solution? To just give up and join in? Although this may appear the better option, Paul would disagree.

Each day, this apostle faced persecution—and not just the "cold shoulder" type, either. His former friends actively sought to silence and even kill him for his newfound faith in Jesus. But instead of just giving in, Paul doubled down, realizing that mankind's approval means nothing in comparison to God's. And because of this, Paul was able to rejoice through the tears of suffering.

No matter how depressed you may feel, you're never alone if God is on your side.

PRAYER STARTER:

*Thank You, God, for making my efforts
worthwhile. When I feel alone, remind
me of Your empowering support.*

FINISHED BUSINESS

*If we confess our sins, he is faithful and
just to forgive us our sins, and to cleanse
us from all unrighteousness.*
1 John 1:9 KJV

. . . .

Ever heard of Martin Luther? If so, you probably know how much of an impact his teachings still have on the church today. When it comes to giants of the faith, Luther was one of the greatest.

But did you know that Martin Luther suffered from crippling anxiety about his own salvation? His internal torment was so intense that many modern psychologists have identified it as a form of religious OCD. Luther had been brought up in a church that emphasized rituals over faith—and so, Luther found himself devastated by a distorted form of God's truth. Instead of rejoicing in God's forgiveness, Martin Luther became terrified of His wrath. He believed his prior sins were too big to be covered by divine grace.

Luther's deep-seated fear soon led to his reevaluation of everything he'd been taught—and a rediscovery of the truth about God as revealed in the Bible. Upon discovering passages like today's verse, Luther found the freedom he thought he'd never obtain. . .and as a result, changed the world.

PRAYER STARTER:

*Thank You, Father, for Your unlimited grace!
Because of Your grace, I don't have to obsess over
my past—Your forgiveness is finished business.*

MUSIC THERAPY

And whenever the tormenting spirit from
God troubled Saul, David would play the
harp. Then Saul would feel better, and the
tormenting spirit would go away.
1 Samuel 16:23 NLT

. . . .

Today's verse is full of mysteries. For starters, why would God send a "tormenting spirit" to Saul? Did God just allow it to happen, or did He send the spirit directly? Was it a test or the result of Saul's disobedience? Was the "spirit" a demon or a mental disorder?

Although we may never know the answers to these questions, one thing is certain: David's calming music provided some much-needed relief for Saul.

Today, countless studies have shown that music is an excellent balm for anxiety. When your chaotic thoughts and feelings build to a crescendo, the simple act of turning on the radio and listening to uplifting, godly music can slow the heart and bring peace to the soul. Music is another one of God's amazing gifts to humanity. And while many people have twisted music to bad purposes, we can use it to both calm ourselves and honor God.

How have you been using the gift of music?

PRAYER STARTER:

Thank You, Father, for music. When I'm drowning
in negative thoughts, remind me of this soothing
form of spiritual and emotional therapy.

CHASING WHALES

But beyond this, my son, be warned:
the writing of many books is endless, and
excessive study is wearying to the body.
ECCLESIASTES 12:12 NASB

. . . .

If you've ever stayed up all night studying for a test, you know how true today's verse is. But this advice doesn't apply only to schoolwork—it can also serve as a guide for anyone who becomes overly obsessed with finding answers, no matter where those answers may lie.

Many people, especially later in life, have gone mad by irrationally pursuing what started out as a mere hobby or topic of interest. Like Captain Ahab hunting the white whale in *Moby Dick*, their entire life soon revolves around attempting to control something that cannot be controlled. Eventually, priorities get all out of whack and healthy minds cave in to severe depression and stress. All this is avoidable, of course, if we remember what the writer of Ecclesiastes said is the true purpose of life: to "fear God and keep His commandments" (12:13 NASB).

God is the one true prize we should run after—every other pursuit amounts to little more than chasing whales.

PRAYER STARTER:

Heavenly Father, thank You for giving
me a solid purpose in life, freeing me
from meaningless obsessions.

THE FEAR OF STUMBLING

For He will give His angels orders concerning you, to protect you in all your ways. On their hands they will lift you up, so that you do not strike your foot against a stone.

PSALM 91:11–12 NASB

. . . .

Today's passage isn't a promise that you'll never stub your toe. Rather, in keeping with the rest of the book of Psalms—which is all poetry—these two verses are rich in symbolism. By using a strong parallel, the psalmist is reassuring his readers that God's angels will protect them from *spiritual* harm. The passage tells us that when our path is littered with dangerous stumbling stones, we don't have to worry about slipping up or falling from grace—God will make sure we pass the test as long as we are willing.

What great news! You don't have to lose sleep tonight, wondering if you'll reject Christ tomorrow. When temptations come, you don't have to be paralyzed with the fear that you might give in. Rather, you can trust in the divine protection that surrounds you, empowering you with the strength to keep living for God.

PRAYER STARTER:

Thank You, Jesus, for Your countless angels that are lifting me up. Help me trust in You for my daily spiritual strength.

NOTHING

For I am persuaded, that neither death, nor life,
nor angels, nor principalities, nor powers, nor things
present, nor things to come, nor height, nor depth, nor
any other creature, shall be able to separate us from
the love of God, which is in Christ Jesus our Lord.
ROMANS 8:38–39 KJV

. . . .

Today's passage is famous for how clearly and boldly
it proclaims the unbreakable nature of God's love.
Nothing—neither the highest archangels in heaven
nor the lowest demons in hell—can shatter it. Paul's
list is lengthy, poignant, and thorough. You can substi-
tute anything on the list with whatever you want—*not*
anxiety, not depression, not loneliness, not fear, not
pain, not despair, not self-hatred, not. . .

Of course, when the fires of anxiety or the gloominess of depression surrounds your soul, remembering
this truth is easier said than done. But by thinking of
these verses on the good days, you can use them as
powerful weapons whenever the forces of darkness
start waging their war.

When you feel cut off from God, separated from His
eternal love, cling to the comforting truth of His Word.

PRAYER STARTER:

Lord, I need You to remind me of Your
unfailing grace and love. It's the only thing
that can pierce my frantic thoughts.

WATER AND FLAME

"When you pass through the waters, I will be with you; and through the rivers, they will not overflow you. When you walk through the fire, you will not be scorched, nor will the flame burn you."

ISAIAH 43:2 NASB

. . . .

Anxiety burns like a cruel flame that starts on your skin and blazes deep into your heart. As the thoughts start churning, your face burns and your hands grow clammy with sweat. . .and then the real pain begins. If anxiety is like fire, depression is like an icy river, enveloping you with pain but sapping your willpower to escape. The longer you stay in this torment, the less likely you are to climb out.

But what does today's verse say about fire and water? That's right: God will help you pass through both. Even at the peak of a panic attack or the lowest point of loneliness and loss, God is with you, promising that you will not only escape unhurt but come out a stronger person.

Today, hold on to God's promises, trusting that He is leading you through the water and flame, protecting you from harm.

PRAYER STARTER:

God, when I pass through the fires and rivers of emotional pain, please take my hand. Shield me with Your love.

DARKNESS NO MORE

The light shines in the darkness, and the
darkness can never extinguish it.
JOHN 1:5 NLT

. . . .

Anxiety and depression can take a person to incredibly dark places—to the point of giving up. It's like being in battle against a faceless foe, who keeps advancing no matter how hard you fight back. At best, it's exhausting; at worst, it's debilitating.

But there's good news: God is more powerful than even the strongest panic attack, and His love runs deeper than the icy blade of despair. When the darkness threatens to take over, trying to suffocate all that is good, God's love pierces through the blackness. . . shining His light of salvation. His promise of eternal life offers hope in the middle of hopelessness, peace amid fear.

When you truly absorb the truths of God's Word, you'll discover a strength you once thought impossible. And as you rise triumphantly with Christ, no power on heaven or earth will be able to stand in your way.

PRAYER STARTER:

Light-bringing God, shine through my darkness and show me the promise of Your hope. I want to feel Your peace in the middle of my pain and despair.

WEEPING FOR A MOMENT

Jesus wept.
JOHN 11:35 NASB

Even as Mary described Lazarus' death to Jesus, He already knew the outcome—Lazarus would rise from the tomb, proving God's power to everyone present. But as Jesus saw Mary and the crowd weeping, something strange happened: He felt their sorrow as well. He personally experienced the soul-crushing weight that comes with loss.

And, in that moment, Jesus wept.

In this life, we cannot avoid grief. It's a fundamentally human experience.

But instead of letting sadness get the upper hand, instead of letting it dominate our emotions and determine our outlook, we can keep sadness in place by focusing on the other side of our existence: joy. And for the Christian, joy isn't hard to find. It's found in everything, even in the middle of unbearable loss. Just as Jesus dried His tears and raised His friend from the grave, we can move forward as well, remembering that our ultimate destination is with God. With a promise like that in our hearts, what room is there for continued sorrow?

PRAYER STARTER:

Thank You, Father, for granting me joy that is stronger than my tears.

NOT GOOD TO BE ALONE

Then the Lord God said, "It is not good for the man to be alone; I will make him a helper suitable for him."
GENESIS 2:18 NASB

. . . .

Sometimes in our loneliness, it's tempting to feel as if no one on earth has ever been as isolated as we are. But today's verse shows that loneliness has been around for a long time—it dates back to the very dawn of humanity.

When Adam was created, he seemingly had it all—a plethora of rich and exotic fruits, a beautiful garden to tend, and a host of animals to keep him company. Only one thing was missing: a human companion. That's right: God knew Adam would never be complete without another person by his side.

Whether you believe it or not, you share Adam's need. You—and everyone else—need human contact to thrive. Everyone needs a friend—whether from school, church, across the street, or within our homes. God has placed us in a world filled with like-minded believers. . .but first, we have to notice them.

Have you found opportunities to enjoy God's gift of friendship?

PRAYER STARTER:

Lord, show me how to form strong relationships with other Christians today.

DEEPER STILL

And the Lord, he it is that doth go before thee;
he will be with thee, he will not fail thee, neither
forsake thee: fear not, neither be dismayed.
DEUTERONOMY 31:8 KJV

. . . .

If anyone in modern times had a reason to sink into the depths of despair, it was Corrie ten Boom. Having lived through the Holocaust in a concentration camp, imprisoned in a filthy, flea-infested cell, she experienced firsthand the deepest depravity to which humans can sink. But even in the middle of such horrific circumstances, Corrie could still feel God.

Instead of giving up on her Christian faith, she read the Bible. (Incidentally, guards were unable to find that since they never entered her cell because of the fleas.) Due to her witness, many other inmates found Christ. As one of these prisoners lay sick and dying, she told Corrie, "There is no pit so deep that He is not deeper still."

If your pit of depression feels impossibly deep, God is deeper still. If your fear runs deep into your soul, God is deeper still. No matter how dark and damp your pit is, God will be by your side. He will never forsake you.

PRAYER STARTER:

Thank You, God, for Your encouraging
and never-failing presence.

EAGERLY AWAITING

*For the eagerly awaiting creation waits for the
revealing of the sons and daughters of God.*
ROMANS 8:19 NASB

. . . .

There's no denying this world has problems. A *lot* of
problems. Natural disasters. Wars. Disease. Poverty.
(Just to name a few.) This imperfect world is shuddering
under its heavy burden—and yet, there will be a day
when all will be made right.

Our worries, our darkest nights of despair, are
merely a sliver of this fallen creation. Our anxieties
and bouts of depression prove to us that this world
is not our home. . .and the hope we have through our
relationship with Jesus is our best weapon to fight
against the darkness.

Without hope, life would have no purpose—all
our worst fears would be true. But with the hope our
heavenly Father brings, we can look beyond our circumstances to the day when we will shine like the sun.

PRAYER STARTER:

*Father God, whenever I feel surrounded
by the anxieties and cares of life, remind
me that even my suffering points me to a
greater hope—because I am Yours.*

WISE COUNSELORS

*Where there is no guidance the people fall, but in
an abundance of counselors there is victory.*
PROVERBS 11:14 NASB

Many teens who struggle with anxiety and depression
see the act of asking for help as a sign of weakness. As
they start to sink into deep despair, they tell themselves,
It's okay. I can fix it on my own.

Of course, this attitude is irrational at best, detrimental at worst. After all, if a guy has a broken arm
or bleeding wound, does he tell himself, *I don't need a
doctor?* Of course not. Yet many with emotional struggles simply refuse to be treated. Not only is an extreme
self-reliance harmful, it goes against God's Word. Many
verses in the Bible—including today's—emphasize the
importance of seeking guidance from the wise. (That's
why Christian counselors exist.)

There's no shame in asking for treatment when
treatment is needed—wise counsel is a gift from God.

PRAYER STARTER:

*Father God, thank You for sending Christians
who can comfort the downtrodden and
soothe the troubled souls. Help me to never
be so proud that I refuse to ask for help.*

PRIVILEGED STATUS

*And fear not them which kill the body, but are
not able to kill the soul: but rather fear him which
is able to destroy both soul and body in hell.*
MATTHEW 10:28 KJV

. . . .

Great, you may be thinking, *what a comforting verse!*
But don't worry: these words from Jesus actually offer
great comfort for God's children.

When you become a Christian, the blood of Jesus
saves you from the threat of hell, so there's no need
to worry about that anymore. In other words, the one
thing Jesus says people should fear (the wrath of God)
is no longer a concern. And as a result, all the other
fears (like the threat of dying) vanish in the light of
God's mercy. It's been said, "You can't kill a Christian—
you can only change his address." And what a glorious
place this new "address" in heaven will be!

So, whatever your fears—disease, the future,
injury, loss, death—remember your status as a child
of God. . .and rejoice!

PRAYER STARTER:

*Lord, I know I have no reason to be anxious, but
it's so hard to keep from focusing on the negatives
in life. Help me to shift my focus away from
my fear and toward the safety of Your love.*

CHAIN OF COMFORT

*Blessed be God. . .who comforteth us in all our
tribulation, that we may be able to comfort
them which are in any trouble, by the comfort
wherewith we ourselves are comforted of God.*

2 CORINTHIANS 1:3–4 KJV

When you're crushed by anxiety, today's scripture has
two applications. The first is obvious: God is able to
comfort us in our darkest hour. When we feel overwhelmed by fear, He's always there, giving us the
strength to carry on. . .and thereby enabling us to
comfort others later.

But for the second application, you have to put
yourself in the shoes of the "others." God often comforts His children through fellow Christians who've
been through similar trials. And chances are you probably know someone who's struggled with anxiety and
depression and come out on top.

So today, don't be afraid to go to that person for
advice. Spill your fears and don't worry about how he
might react. People who've "been there" understand
others who are currently struggling—there's no room
for judgment or mockery.

When God's children encourage each other, it
creates a chain of comfort, providing hope that goes
on and on.

PRAYER STARTER:

*Thank You, Father, for the comfort You provide—
both directly and from others who love You.*

MADE WHOLE

He will take our weak mortal bodies and change
them into glorious bodies like his own.
PHILIPPIANS 3:21 NLT

. . . .

Today's promise is one of the most amazing in the whole Bible. Not only will heaven be free from external threats and distressing situations, but it will also be a place where our bodies and minds are transformed to perfection.

No longer will imbalances exist in the brain—anxiety and depression will be wiped from our minds forever. No longer will we feel the emptiness of loneliness and despair—endless companionship with our Creator will fill us with eternal joy. No longer will the future seem threatening or uncertain—we will be locked in one eternal, blissful moment, unaffected by the passage of time.

So, the next time anxiety tries to take over, distorting reality and attempting to make you believe things will never get better, let today's verse be your refuge. Focus on God's eternal goodness and love. Look past this broken world toward the perfect world that lies beyond.

Pain is temporary, but your new life will last forever.

PRAYER STARTER:

Remind me, God, of the perfect body and
mind that await me in heaven. I look forward
to the day I'm made completely whole.

ONE OR THE OTHER

*Be thankful in all circumstances, for this is
God's will for you who belong to Christ Jesus.*
1 Thessalonians 5:18 NLT

Recent research has proven once again that God knows
what He's talking about. Today's verse, for instance,
tells us that His will is for us to give thanks in *all* circumstances—even the ones that fuel our anxiety. And
now, scientists have discovered a shocking truth: It
seems gratitude and anxiety can't coexist. When one
is in play, the other has to leave.

How amazing is that? Just the simple act of thanking
God can—at least in the moment—eliminate your anxiety. The hard part, of course, comes with generating the
willpower to be grateful when anxiety comes knocking.
But when you intentionally live with a thankful mindset,
you'll find gratitude begins to come naturally, whenever
you need it the most.

Today, whether you're at peace or experiencing the
worst stress of your life, start counting your blessings.
Don't try to block out the anxious thoughts by yourself—the mere act of thanksgiving will do that for you.

Thank God for the gift of gratitude.

PRAYER STARTER:

*Thank You, generous Father, for giving me all sorts
of reasons to rejoice—this wonderful world, the
kind people in my life, and Your gift of salvation.*

WORKOUT ROUTINE

For this light momentary affliction is preparing for
us an eternal weight of glory beyond all comparison.
2 CORINTHIANS 4:17 ESV

. . . .

Paul really loved his "workout routine" metaphors, and today's verse is no exception. Here, the apostle paints a picture of a dedicated weight lifter who raises small amounts each day until he is strong enough to take on the final challenge. In Paul's illustration, the final challenge is heaven itself!

Paul seems to be saying that eternity with God is such a weighty concept that it takes a gradual strengthening process before we can handle it. But obtaining this strength doesn't come easily—it comes through suffering and trials. This can include anything from physical disease to emotional pain. All are necessary to remove our confidence in ourselves and push us onward to the blessed life that awaits.

So today, don't give up in your fight against anxiety and depression. . .but also don't forget that these trials, as hard as they may seem, will be worth it in the end.

PRAYER STARTER:

Lord, don't let me collapse under the pressure of
stress and sadness. Instead, build my spiritual
strength, preparing me for eternity with You.

TOO ASHAMED TO PRAY

When Jesus heard this, he told them, "Healthy people don't need a doctor—sick people do."
MARK 2:17 NLT

. . . .

Have you ever felt so mentally scattered that you were ashamed at the thought of praying? Maybe doubts and fears and terrible thoughts are rushing through your mind, making you feel unclean and unworthy of God's attention.

If so, remember: Nothing could be further from the truth. When our brains are afflicted—either from sin or from the torment of our own thoughts—Jesus isn't ashamed of you, nor does He try to avoid you. No, He's the Great Physician, willing to use His infinite power for the good of all who ask. He won't push you away—your flaws, fears, and insecurities are the very things that draw Him *to* you! He came to earth for the sick, poor, and downtrodden. . .and to this day, He hasn't changed a bit.

Go to Jesus with your anxiety and despair. He's on the lookout for someone to comfort today.

PRAYER STARTER:

Thank You, Jesus, for Your healing power. Help me to never be afraid to run to You, even when it feels like I'm not good enough to pray.

61

HOPE IS REAL

We know that God makes all things work together for the good of those who love Him and are chosen to be a part of His plan.
ROMANS 8:28 NLV

. . . .

Today's verse is a comfort for anyone who is discouraged by today's disappointments or fears tomorrow.

Without looking at the bigger picture—without an understanding of God's love—life becomes merely a string of events, some happy and others devastating. There's no rhyme or reason to it all: stuff just happens, and we'd do well to take it all with a straight backbone and a stiff upper lip.

But thankfully, that's not how it all works. For God's children, everything *does* happen for a reason. So rather than accept defeat and meaninglessness, we can accept a much greater truth: God is working our pain into a masterpiece that will be revealed at the end. His plan, while we may not "get it" right now, is hurtling us forward into a brighter tomorrow. If it takes days, weeks, months, years—even a lifetime—we *will* see the purpose behind our suffering. . .and we'll praise God when that day arrives.

PRAYER STARTER:

With You, Lord, there are no accidents. Teach me how to look beyond today's unpleasant events and toward Your perfect plan.

OPEN THE CAGE

And after you have suffered a little while, the God of all grace, who has called you to his eternal glory in Christ, will himself restore, confirm, strengthen, and establish you.
1 PETER 5:10 ESV

In the enduring classic *The Pilgrim's Progress*, Christian finds himself locked up by a giant named Despair. Each day, Despair visits Christian's cage, viciously beats him, and then walks away, leaving behind the tools Christian would need to end his own life.

But as Christian reaches the limits of his endurance, he remembers: he holds the key of Promise! Using this miraculous key, he opens the lock and escapes Despair's gloomy castle at last.

This poignant allegory shows how powerful God's promises are to His children. When you're blindsided by loneliness and the fear that life will never improve, remember today's scripture. Instead of giving in to the dark thoughts that attack you, try to imagine a day when God's light will triumph once and for all. This isn't just a fantasy—it's a solid reality, spoken by Truth Himself.

Today, let God's promises open your cage of despair.

PRAYER STARTER:
Lord, thank You for promising a hope that will outlast my hopelessness—a peace that will conquer my fear.

IN THE PIT

I waited patiently for the LORD; and he inclined unto me, and heard my cry. He brought me up also out of an horrible pit, out of the miry clay, and set my feet upon a rock, and established my goings.
PSALM 40:1–2 KJV

. . . .

The psalmist wrote today's passage as he healed from a deep depression. His words came from a place of relief—from sincere gratitude for a long-awaited reprieve from suffering.

If you're going through a time of depression, the psalmist's joy might seem strange or even off-putting. It feels as if you've never experienced these positive emotions. . .and never will. But you can know that's a lie. Even in your darkest moments, you can take comfort in the fact that things will indeed get better. God won't leave you in the pit forever—He's guaranteed to lift you out as long as you cling to Him, waiting patiently for His rescue.

When your face forgets how to smile, don't worry. If joy seems out of reach, know that it will come in due time. Hold on till the breaking of the dawn.

PRAYER STARTER:

Father, please rescue me from this pit I'm in. Help me to never give in or stop climbing upward toward Your outstretched hand.

INFINITE VALUE

*For you formed my inward parts; you knitted me
together in my mother's womb. I praise you, for
I am fearfully and wonderfully made. Wonderful
are your works; my soul knows it very well.*
PSALM 139:13–14 ESV

One of the most sinister weapons in depression's arsenal is the lie that you are some sort of mistake. Your brain will scream this lie every chance it gets: in class, at lunch, at the dinner table with your family, in the middle of your chores, on vacation, in the car, on your bed late at night.

This lie can be almost impossible to overcome on your own. But the first step toward fighting back is recognizing the lie for what it is: *a lie*. While your brain is saying you have no value, your mind and soul can know that's just not true. How? By remembering today's scripture.

You were not a mistake. God planned and eagerly anticipated your life before the foundation of the world. Jesus died to grant you a place in His kingdom. . .and He rose again to be your personal Savior. No matter what you think, your life has infinite value.

Are you living out this truth today?

PRAYER STARTER:

*Lord, remind me of today's scripture
whenever I forget my purpose.*

GOD'S RIGHT HAND

"Don't be afraid, for I am with you.
Don't be discouraged, for I am your God.
I will strengthen you and help you. I will hold
you up with my victorious right hand."
ISAIAH 41:10 NLT

. . . .

Are you worried about that test tomorrow? That presentation next week? That new school you're getting ready to attend? That sickness that's going around? That friend who's been acting unkindly to you? That relationship that seems to be falling apart?

If so, it may seem cliché to say, "Don't be afraid." After all, that's easier said than done. Fear is a natural (sometimes brutal) response that takes loads of effort and occasionally help to overcome. But today's verse gives you reason for fighting back against fear—a motive for resisting the lie that you are destined for failure. As long as God is holding you up with His right hand (a symbol of His infinite power and protection), there's no need to fret about tomorrow; instead, you are free to pursue His peace.

Aren't you glad that God's promises are more powerful than your uncertainties?

PRAYER STARTER:

Thank You, almighty God, for holding me up
when I need Your strength. Be with me as I face
down the enemies of fear and depression.

MAKE MY DAY

This is the day which the LORD hath made;
we will rejoice and be glad in it.
PSALM 118:24 KJV

. . . .

Today's verse is extremely familiar. . .and it remains one of the most powerful statements in the book of Psalms.

Imagine God as He formed the universe from nothing. Not only did He create every physical thing that surrounds us, He created time itself. He designed those chunks of time between the rising and setting of the sun, which we call days. Before He spoke reality into existence, He knew exactly what would occur today—its stresses, joys, and boredoms—and He literally made time for everything to happen.

Today, try moving your thoughts from the stress of the moment to focus on the moment itself. In other words, give thanks to God for the world you inhabit. . .the air you breathe. . .the very time through which your life is passing. God has not only made today good—He has *made today*, so it's good by default (Genesis 1:4).

Don't hesitate to thank God for making your day!

PRAYER STARTER:

Lord, when I stop to think of how powerful
and good You are, my stress takes a backseat
to gratitude. I can't thank You enough for
creating this world that I call home.

WHEN THE WORLD BURNS

*The grass withers, the flower fades, but the
word of our God will stand forever.*
ISAIAH 40:8 ESV

Having a panic attack is the mental equivalent of looking
into a fun-house mirror. . .only there's nothing "fun"
about it. The more you consider your situation, the
more distorted the image becomes. It feels like you are
shrinking and falling as everything around you balloons
into crazy proportions. Even a beautiful sunset seems
to glow ominously.

During such an attack, it can feel like the world is
ending, like everything you know and love is on fire,
withering in the heat of despair. But whenever you feel
this way, let today's verse be your anchor. Even in this
kaleidoscope of confusion, God's Word remains the
one constant you can trust. It's true that everything
around you will one day pass away. . .but His truth is
the sole exception.

So today, in your churning sea of uncertainty,
cling to God's promises. His love is a raft that will carry
you through the tempest and toward a hope that will
never pass away.

PRAYER STARTER:

*Father, whenever I lose my trust in everything
else, give me the strength to trust Your Word.
Guide me to safety with Your eternal truth.*

FORGIVE YOURSELF

Those who look to him are radiant,
and their faces shall never be ashamed.
PSALM 34:5 ESV

Do you struggle with shame? Does an already-confessed sin in your past haunt your thoughts? Maybe you were unkind to someone at school or you took part in an activity you're not proud of. Now you find yourself obsessing over it, trying desperately to make things right. Or, less dramatically, uncertainty about God's forgiveness lingers in the back of your mind, surfacing during moments of stress and depression.

If so, now's the time to work through some unresolved guilt. Today's verse tells us that those who follow God are "radiant," having no reason to feel ashamed. Why? Because God's forgiveness is absolute. Once He forgives you, your sin is not only covered but completely erased from your record. Even the worst sinner, at the moment he receives God's grace, becomes just as righteous as the sinless Jesus! There's no need to dwell on your old sins—every hint of past imperfections on your soul has been scrubbed clean, leaving nothing but a polished slate.

Have you embraced God's amazing forgiveness?

PRAYER STARTER:

God, I know You've already forgiven
me. . .so now help me forgive myself.

BEING FOLLOWED

*Surely goodness and mercy shall follow
me all the days of my life: and I will dwell
in the house of the LORD for ever.*
PSALM 23:6 KJV

· ·

At their worst, anxiety and depression can feel like
nighttime stalkers, hiding in the shadowy corners of
your mind, waiting for an opportunity to attack. Even
when you're having a good day, these faceless foes
linger in the back of your mind—and fill your gut with
unease.

Well, today's verse says that if you're a child of God,
two other forces follow you wherever you go. These
"stalkers," however, aren't bent on your destruction—
they're dedicated to your safety and spiritual well-
being. That's right: goodness and mercy are trailing
close on your heels, protecting you from the devil's
schemes.

Like spiritual bodyguards, God's goodness and
mercy travel in the glow of His holiness, surrounding
your life with blessings. Even when anxiety strikes and
depression slips in from the back, goodness and mercy
are there to make sure your soul is safe and sound.

PRAYER STARTER:

*Everlasting God, protect me with Your
goodness and mercy. When I'm assailed by
my own mind, remind me that You're fighting
on my behalf. My soul is safe with You.*

FEELS GOOD TO GIVE

"In everything I showed you that by working hard in this way you must help the weak and remember the words of the Lord Jesus, that He Himself said, 'It is more blessed to give than to receive.'"
ACTS 20:35 NASB

. . . .

We Christians in America have been spoiled. While for centuries God's children have endured suffering, poverty, and oppression, many of us today are protected and upheld by the laws of the land. Paradoxically, in our wealthy and peaceful culture, anxiety seems to be growing at a rapid pace. Why? It's complicated. . .but at least part of the reason stems from the truth in today's verse.

When our lives are filled with material things, it's easy to turn our focus inward. But when we introduce generosity into the picture, we move the focus from ourselves to the needs of others. Once we're giving, it's hard to fixate on our personal problems. Anxiety and depression may still exist, but they'll become much easier to manage.

Today, think of a person who needs your help. . .then help. You'll be surprised at how good your acts of kindness will feel.

PRAYER STARTER:
Lord, don't let my fears get in the way of my purpose.

UNKNOWABLE

"Do not worry about tomorrow. Tomorrow will have its own worries. The troubles we have in a day are enough for one day."
MATTHEW 6:34 NLV

As Jesus spoke the words of today's verse, He was no doubt aware of the intense suffering He'd endure on the cross. He realized the cruelty of the road ahead.

Jesus knew how easy it was to focus on tomorrow. . .but He also knew how pointless worrying would be. Today's concerns—instructing the eager multitudes, teaching His disciples to walk in God's kingdom, enduring the mockery of His enemies—were enough to keep Him busy. He took things one day at a time, trusting in His Father to provide strength for the future.

It's no different for us. In fact, we have it even better! Jesus knew the full extent of His future pain. . .but all we know is that our future lies in God's hands. So when anxiety sneaks up to whisper fears about an unknowable future, ask Jesus to help you take this life day by day.

PRAYER STARTER:

Lord Jesus, take my focus off of tomorrow, which I can't control, and onto my present choices, which I can.

ENDURING LOVE

Love never gives up, never loses faith, is always
hopeful, and endures through every circumstance.
1 CORINTHIANS 13:7 NLT

When you think of love, what comes to mind? Your relationship with Mom or Dad? A romantic picnic with that special girl? A warm feeling that drives away all doubt or negativity?

While all these things are aspects of love, they're not the entirety. A fuller picture can be found in today's verse. Love is endurance in the middle of the pain. Love is trusting God when it seems like your life is falling apart. Love is holding tightly to the hope that all will someday be made well. Love is looking upward with teary eyes and waiting for the light to come.

In short, love can be hard. When you're a teen, your emotions surge all over the place—you may feel joyful one second, sad the next. But love rests at the center, solid and unchanging. It provides some much-needed stability and even defines who you are.

No matter how you're feeling right now, ask God for the strength to keep loving.

PRAYER STARTER:

I love You, Father. Please help this love to survive
the hard times I'm walking through. I want to come
out of this stronger and still clinging to You.

MISPLACED FAITH

*"No eye has seen, no ear has heard,
and no mind has imagined what God has
prepared for those who love him."*
1 CORINTHIANS 2:9 NLT

. . . .

Anxiety can sometimes feel like you're stumbling through a dark room, unsure of where you're going or what might lurk in the shadows. You can't see the threat, but you just *know* it's there—in that moment, you believe in your heart that something bad is about to happen.

Well, today's verse tells us to flip that misplaced faith on its head. In a sense, we're all walking through a dark and uncertain world. . .but instead of evil waiting for us around every corner, we have God's unimaginable blessings to look forward to. We can't see them now, but we can *know* they're here. Why? Because that's what the Bible promises, and it never lies.

By constantly dwelling on the good things God has in store for you, you'll find yourself eager to embrace what happens next. No more stumbling through this world—run with arms wide open to your heavenly Father.

PRAYER STARTER:

Lord God, I can't wait to see what heaven will be like, and I'm eager to enjoy the blessings You've prepared for me in this life. Give me faith in You, not in my fear.

STRENGTH IN NUMBERS

Resist [the devil], firm in your faith, knowing that
the same kinds of suffering are being experienced
by your brotherhood throughout the world.
1 PETER 5:9 ESV

Not all emotional struggles come directly from Satan—many are caused either by trauma or chemical imbalances in the brain. But even though the attacks on your mind are just as physical as they are spiritual, the devil would love nothing more than to see you crumble under their weight. That's why today's verse tells you to fight back and never give in.

And how does Peter say you should do this? By bonding with fellow Christians who've been through similar trials. That's right: deep human connection with those who understand you can be more powerful than all the therapists and medicines (and well-meaning platitudes) put together.

So today, if you're feeling anguish, start by surrounding yourself with believers who've been through the same depths and emerged victorious. Listen to their stories, learn from them, heed their advice.

Anxiety and depression are fearsome foes, but remember this: there's strength in numbers.

PRAYER STARTER:

Lord Jesus, open my eyes to see other Christians—
whether teens or older adults—who've walked
the same road I'm walking now. Then open
my ears to learn from their stories.

SMALL PROBLEMS, BIG SOLUTION

Do not worry. Learn to pray about everything.
Give thanks to God as you ask Him for what you need.
PHILIPPIANS 4:6 NLV

Today's verse gives us a hefty challenge: "Learn to pray about everything." At first, some prayers might seem awkward or even unnecessary. *Why would God care about my toothache?* you may think. *And does it really matter if tomorrow's science test goes well?*

The answer might surprise you: the outcome of these prayers is often less important than the simple fact that you prayed. Why? Because by praying about even the small things, you are training your mind to trust God in everything. Pretty soon, such dependence will become second nature to you, preparing you for whenever the "big one" comes. Gradually, your fears about the future will be replaced with a million tiny prayers of gratitude as you see God come through time and time again. He becomes not just a crutch you lean on when things get rough but a constant companion who is always happy to help with even the smallest of tasks.

That's what it's like to truly walk with God!

PRAYER STARTER:

Lord, teach me to bring all my cares—
big and small—to lay at Your feet.

WARTIME BELIEVERS

The LORD will also be a stronghold for the oppressed, a stronghold in times of trouble.

PSALM 9:9 NASB

. . . .

Fighting anxiety and depression isn't something you do by just ignoring them or wishing them away. No, it may take every ounce of your willpower to stand up and use your God-given tools to fight back. When you're in the thick of emotion, this process feels less like a behavioral therapy session and more like an all-out war.

Today's verse was written for wartime believers—Christians who are giving their all against the forces of evil, doubt, and fear. In the heat of battle, it's easy to forget where your true strength comes from. But the psalmist's words are here to remind you that God is your refuge.

When you feel like you can't go on, like sadness and fear are winning, retreat into the safety of God's Word. Focus your mind on His power and the promises He's made to you. . .then use the strength these truths bring to keep fighting.

God offers you a safe space today. Take Him up on the offer!

PRAYER STARTER:

Lord, give me the wisdom to rest in Your truth whenever I feel like I can't go on. I know You'll never let me be defeated.

CARRY THE TORCH

I have set the LORD always before me; because
he is at my right hand, I shall not be shaken.
PSALM 16:8 ESV

. . . .

All through the Bible, God's truth is compared to a light that brightens our path in a dark world. And in today's verse, we see that God Himself is our guide through life.

Notice something important about the wording of this verse. The psalm writer himself has chosen to set God before him. Being a Christian and living in the light of God's promises doesn't just happen naturally or by accident—it takes willpower and unchanging dedication to see beyond our circumstances. Like an explorer using a torch to illuminate a deep, black cave, we must remember to hold up God and His Word so that His light can pierce the darkness in our minds and hearts.

Have you decided to set God before you today? Are you continually making that decision, trusting it will pay off in the end? If so, don't give up—there's an eternal light at the end of the tunnel.

PRAYER STARTER:

Lord, remind me to use the light You've given
me to fight against my negative thoughts.
With You by my side, I will never be shaken.

DESERT SHADE

*One who dwells in the shelter of the Most High
will lodge in the shadow of the Almighty.*

PSALM 91:1 NASB

. . . .

In 1994, a man named Mauro Prosperi participated
in one of the most extreme challenges imaginable: a
six-day footrace across the Sahara Desert. Perhaps
unsurprisingly, this challenge soon came with a life-
threatening catastrophe—in Mauro's case, an unexpected sandstorm in the middle of the fourth day.
Blinded by the blowing, blistering sand, Mauro soon
lost sight of the trail. Once the winds subsided, he
found himself in a terrifying predicament: he was lost,
exposed to the harshest elements on earth with nothing
but the scalding dunes to keep him company.

But in the distance, Mauro noticed something: a
small building, erected long ago as a shrine, jutting
from the dunes. Even when he ran out of food and
water, this building offered him one crucial, life-saving
element over the next several days: shade.

Today's verse says that God is your shade—your
hiding place from the sands of fear and despair. Even
when your world is a desert, God's promises can shield
you from the heat.

PRAYER STARTER:

*Thank You, Father, for providing relief in this brutal,
unrelenting desert. When my mouth is parched and
my feet are burning, may I find solace in Your love.*

WHAT REMAINS

Three things will last forever—faith, hope, and love—and the greatest of these is love.
1 CORINTHIANS 13:13 NLT

· ·

Anxiety attacks are fearsome because they're so effective at stealing the greatest natural weapon we possess: our clear thinking. In the heat of panic, we forget things we've learned and assume the pain will last forever. In that sense, the first attack is no worse than the fiftieth—the feeling of being forever doomed is as potent as ever.

That's why today's verse is so useful for us. It promises that what lasts forever is not our fear but our faith, hope, and love. As long as some memory of these three remains, you can rest assured, knowing that even the hottest fires can't burn them away. Clinging to your love for God—and your trust in His love for you—will ensure your survival, no matter how intense your emotions become. And when the dust settles, your soul will emerge stronger than ever.

PRAYER STARTER:

Lord God, whenever anxiety or panic grips my mind, remind me of these things: faith, hope, and love. Help me remember that even the worst emotional assault can't steal my relationship with You.

INFINITY TO ONE

What shall we then say to these things?
If God be for us, who can be against us?
ROMANS 8:31 KJV

. . . .

As finite humans, it's only natural to be afraid of what other people can do to us. But because we serve an all-powerful God, our old natural fears are now out of style, replaced by a supernatural strength that merely absorbs the worst of the nonbelievers' assaults. They can tease and mock us and even cause physical harm—but they can't steal the one thing that matters the most: our souls.

Countless believers have faced the worst the world has to offer and, with God's help, came through victorious. Even those early Christians who were killed for their faith now stand glorified in heaven, waiting to see God's final judgment poured out on the wicked (Revelation 6:10).

So if people bully you for your faith, who cares? There's no need to feel anxious or depressed about what others say. As long as God is on your side, it's never a fair fight. The odds are stacked in your favor—infinity to one.

PRAYER STARTER:

Almighty God, thank You for giving me a reason not to fear the opinions of others. When it comes to living out my faith, help me to be courageous, not afraid.

PUBLIC IMAGE

So God created man in his own image,
in the image of God he created him;
male and female he created them.
GENESIS 1:27 ESV

. . . .

If you're like most teens, you care about what other people think of you. Maybe you feel self-conscious about wearing old clothes. Maybe you're trying to impress your peers by your words or actions. While there's nothing wrong with wanting people to like you, trouble arises when you attempt to change who you are.

You weren't made in the image of the cool guy down the street. You weren't made in the image of that social media star you're emulating. You weren't even made in the image of your closest friend. All these "images" are just facades, masking the true image in which everyone (including you) was made—the image of *God*.

Our self-image—our identity—belongs in the will of the God who made us, not in the whims and trends of a superficial, distractable culture. Chasing the wrong image creates turmoil as we stray further from our true purpose.

PRAYER STARTER:

God, help me live in Your image, obeying
You over the fashions of this culture.

NO MISTAKES

*Then the LORD said to him, "Who has made
man's mouth? Who makes him mute, or deaf,
or seeing, or blind? Is it not I, the LORD?"*
EXODUS 4:11 ESV

. . . .

Do you ever see yourself as insignificant—as a mistake-prone third wheel who doesn't belong? Have you ever stayed awake at night questioning whether your life has meaning? Have your insecurities painted a disgusting picture of yourself in your own mind, a taunting portrait of incompetence?

If you suffer from depression, the chances are high that at least one of these tormenting thoughts has crossed your mind. The ugly thing about depression is that it tries to disfigure the core of your being. While pride attempts to elevate your self-importance, depression wants to erase it altogether, masking self-hatred in pretend humility. . .all while ironically focusing your attention even further inward.

Today, let this verse counteract depression's lies. God designed you with purpose. In His eyes, you're vital to His ultimate plan. When He created the universe and designed its course, He formed you as a key player.

By serving God and following His will, you are, quite literally, changing the world.

PRAYER STARTER:

God, help me to see the value I have in Your eyes.

THE MOST POWERFUL WEAPON

"No weapon that is formed against you will succeed; and you will condemn every tongue that accuses you in judgment."
ISAIAH 54:17 NASB

. . . .

When most people read this verse, they think of enemies' hateful words and the best efforts of Satan to confound God's children. But as anyone who suffers with anxiety and depression can attest, the most destructive weapons often come from within our own mind. Insecurity, self-loathing, doubt, fear, loneliness, anger, bitterness, regret, and trauma can crawl up out of the slimy well in the back of your brain, slithering their way into the forefront of your thoughts.

But today's verse says that the worst weapons—even the ones of your own making—will not succeed. . . as long as you stand in God's will. In the midst of this merciless condemning onslaught, you can flip the tables, reminding your sinister alter-ego of the power of God's grace.

No child of God has to face his own mind alone. God's love is the most powerful weapon of all, and it's already won the war.

PRAYER STARTER:

Forgiving God, thank You for wiping my slate clean. Clearly, the voices in the back of my mind don't understand Your all-encompassing forgiveness, so give me the courage to stand up to them today.

INCOMPREHENSIBLE

*And the peace of God, which surpasses
all comprehension, will guard your
hearts and minds in Christ Jesus.*

PHILIPPIANS 4:7 NASB

. . . .

Do you struggle to comprehend God's master plan for
your life? Have you ever obsessed over what comes
next, worrying that you might do the wrong thing? Are
you afraid of the future? If so, today's verse provides
good news.

In that hazy space where our doubts and uneasy
feelings lie, God's peace begins. But we'll never obtain
this peace by understanding the future. Peace comes
when we understand that we do not understand.

What exactly is this peace grounded in? God's
wisdom and sovereignty. Even when we don't know
what's best, we can know that *God* knows. . .and He
also knows how to bring about our good.

The next time you feel your pulse quickening over
what lies ahead, don't try fighting against the uncertainty—embrace it and receive God's peace of mind.

PRAYER STARTER:

*Thank You, all-knowing God, for making me
realize that it's okay not to understand.
Allow me to revel in Your incomprehensible peace.*

MOSTLY DEAD

In journeyings often, in perils of waters, in perils of robbers, in perils by mine own countrymen, in perils by the heathen, in perils in the city, in perils in the wilderness, in perils in the sea, in perils among false brethren. . . . If I must needs glory, I will glory of the things which concern mine infirmities.

2 CORINTHIANS 11:26, 30 KJV

. . . .

In the timeless classic *The Princess Bride*, Westley, the main hero of the story, is tortured nearly to death by the evil villain Humperdinck. Finding Westley in such a state, his fellow travelers take him to an eccentric healer named Miracle Max. "It just so happens that your friend here is only mostly dead," Max proclaims. "There's a big difference between mostly dead and all dead. Mostly dead is slightly alive."

The apostle Paul knew what it was like to feel "mostly dead." He'd been beaten, shipwrecked, and stoned to within an inch of his life. But even in the midst of extreme suffering—both physical and emotional—he knew that these trials were making his faith stronger than ever. In his eyes, mostly dead meant *fully* alive!

PRAYER STARTER:

Lord, please let me come out from this period of anxiety stronger than ever. Use this pain to draw me closer to You.

POOR IN SPIRIT

"Blessed are the poor in spirit,
for theirs is the kingdom of heaven."
MATTHEW 5:3 ESV

. . . .

You may think that nothing is more harmful to a person's faith than anxiety. And yes, while unchecked fear can eventually hurt a person's spiritual walk, there's one thing that's even worse: complacency.

Complacency means simply not caring. No longer are you looking up, reaching for a better life, or striving to improve; rather, you tell yourself, *I'll stay right here and never change—it's easier that way.* Faith, however, is no stagnant pool—it's a swift river, forever flowing toward the ocean of eternity.

That's why today's verse suggests that the "poor in spirit" are closer to God. While God wants to heal our brokenness, He'll often use it first to grow us into the warriors we were meant to be. Sometimes, the only way to climb a mountain is by first walking through the valley of the shadow of death.

No matter what you're suffering through today, rest assured: It won't last forever. God is always leading you closer to home.

PRAYER STARTER:

Thank You, Father, for promising that You
have a purpose for my suffering.

FREE SPIRIT

Now I want you to know, brothers and sisters,
that my circumstances have turned out for
the greater progress of the gospel.
PHILIPPIANS 1:12 NASB

. . . .

When Paul wrote the words above, he was in prison. . .which you'd think wouldn't exactly be the best place for the gospel to spread.

But you'd be wrong.

You see, even though Paul was in chains, his influence was growing each day. Why? Because he trusted in God in the midst of his bondage, thus serving as an inspiration for everyone who saw him. His body was in prison, but his spirit was utterly, indisputably free.

Perhaps you feel imprisoned—not by literal chains but by the fear in your mind, the endless cycles of depression. Maybe you've tried to escape, with little to no success. If so, don't quit trying! Fight against these chains with every weapon in your pack—prayer, the support of family and friends, doctors and medications if appropriate.

But most importantly, *keep the faith*. When others see your perseverance in the face of despair, they'll be inspired by your dedication. Even in your darkest prison, your soul will find true freedom.

PRAYER STARTER:

God, when the chains of depression and anxiety cling to my wrists, help me to hold even more tightly to You.

PERFECT EXAMPLE

For it was fitting that he, for whom and by whom all things exist, in bringing many sons to glory, should make the founder of their salvation perfect through suffering.
HEBREWS 2:10 ESV

. . . .

A profound sense of sadness at the death of a friend. A frantic prayer for God to change the future, if possible. Fear so great that it produces sweat like drops of blood—raw anguish unlike any the world has seen.

Who do you think these images describe? That's right: Jesus.

If the perfect Son of God endured so much mental anguish during His earthly life, what does that say about our own suffering? Is it rational to believe that in order to be "good Christians," we can't feel any fear or sense of loss in the face of disaster? Many people think so. . .but maybe these people don't know their own Savior as well as they claim.

Of course, God wants us to move out of our anxiety and depression, not suffer in it for ages. But ignoring these emotions isn't our way of escape. By coming to grips with our humanity and trusting God to help us, we can begin to progress toward a brighter tomorrow.

PRAYER STARTER:

Thank You, Jesus, for being the perfect example for me as I struggle.

A HIDDEN LIFE

*Yes, and everyone who wants to live a godly
life in Christ Jesus will suffer persecution.*
2 TIMOTHY 3:12 NLT

You may never have heard of Franz Jägerstätter—an Austrian farmer who objected to Hitler's rule even as his friends sold their consciences for safety. Because he refused to swear allegiance to Hitler, he was imprisoned and eventually sent to the guillotine. His last words were "I am completely bound in inner union with the Lord."

After his death, Franz's name slipped into obscurity. . .but his story wasn't over yet. Decades later, an author dug up records of his sacrifice and brought his devotion to public attention. And eventually, a poignant movie was produced about his sacrifice: *A Hidden Life*.

When you feel like the only one who's still serving God, loneliness and worry seem unavoidable. You may even think all your efforts have gone in vain. But take heart: God is still on your side. Like Franz Jägerstätter, you can stay sane in a crazy world by anchoring your hope to God's will. And years after the world's persecutions fade, your faith will be the one thing that remains.

PRAYER STARTER:

*God, when I'm discouraged by those who
mock my faith, please replace my fear
with endurance, reminding me that Your
recognition is all that matters.*

WATCH WHAT YOU EAT

Or do you not know that your body is a
temple of the Holy Spirit within you? . . .
Therefore glorify God in your body.
1 CORINTHIANS 6:19–20 NASB

Today's passage specifically discusses immorality, but it can be applied to a variety of life issues. One common application comes in the form of our dietary choices. Since our body is a temple, it only makes sense to treat it well.

But your diet doesn't just include the foods you eat. Think about it: Your brain is just as much a part of your body as your stomach, so whatever you feed it will affect you in one way or another. If you choose to feed your mind with inspiring art, the beauty of God's creation, and the truths in His Word, it will thrive. But if your diet consists of toxic social media, mean-spirited humor, and ungodly attitudes. . .well, that's the mental equivalent of eating junk food for breakfast, lunch, and dinner. Those things will inevitably take a toll on your health, making your escape from anxiety and depression even harder.

What's on your plate?

PRAYER STARTER:

Lord, when it comes to what I feed my
brain, help me to watch what I eat.

LISTEN UP!

The way of a fool is right in his own eyes,
but a wise man listens to advice.
PROVERBS 12:15 ESV

. . . .

I'm strong—I don't need any help! Therapy and counseling are for wimps. I'll figure things out my own way!
Today's verse is brutally honest about people with such a mindset: they're fools. The more we learn about neuroscience and mental health, the more we learn how complex our amazing brains are. In many cases, it takes a mechanic to fix a car—and it often takes a wise and godly counselor to help fix issues in your mind. Seeking help for anxiety and depression isn't a sign of weakness—it shows humility and strength.

God has provided fellow believers who take mental health seriously and strive to use their expertise to make the world a better place. How arrogant we are to refuse that help when we need it! Today, don't be afraid to reach out for assistance. God is right beside you, leading you to solutions He's already prepared.

PRAYER STARTER:

Lord, guide me to be more open to advice from
those who can help. Thank You for providing
such people to assist in our struggles.

DON'T LOOK DOWN

The Lord God is my strength,
and He has made my feet like deer's feet,
and has me walk on my high places.
HABAKKUK 3:19 NASB

. . . .

One of the most common phobias is the fear of heights. Pretty much everyone struggles with it to some degree—and that's why today's verse is so powerful.

Whether you're afraid of spiders or suffer a crippling fear that you'll never measure up in life, God can lead you through the fear and bring you out unharmed. Even if the world seems to be swirling around you—if you're feeling lightheaded and weak in the knees—God is firmly holding your arm, leading you to the top of His mountain of peace.

Today, resist the urge to look down. Don't focus on what could go wrong, but dwell on the reassuring promises in God's Word. Never be content to stay on the ground—go with God to new heights.

PRAYER STARTER:

Lord, thank You for giving me the courage to step out on faith. I know that as long as I'm holding on to You and You're holding on to me, there is never a danger of my slipping.

STRESSFUL SITUATIONS

For God hath not given us the spirit of fear;
but of power, and of love, and of a sound mind.
2 TIMOTHY 1:7 KJV

. . . .

Some Christians take today's verse as proof that any anxiety you feel comes directly from the devil—so it's a sin to let fear into your mind. But a simple glance at the context of this verse shows this just isn't the case.

Paul isn't speaking here of generalized anxiety—a condition often caused by chemical imbalances and other biological issues. Rather, he's talking about the anxiety you feel when it comes to living for God. Whenever you face opposition for your faith, it's tempting to give in to fear and worry about what lies ahead. But when you take today's verse to heart, you realize that's the opposite of how God wants you to live.

Today, ask God to replace your fears with courage—ask for confidence instead of insecurity. Place your faith in Him, not in yourself, and watch as His strength flows through your life.

> ### PRAYER STARTER:
>
> *Lord, thank You for giving me a spirit*
> *that can withstand the stresses of*
> *today and the fear of tomorrow.*

FLESHLY SORROWS

For to set the mind on the flesh is death, but to set the mind on the Spirit is life and peace.
ROMANS 8:6 ESV

This world can be a rough place. Wars break out, innocent lives are lost, poverty surges, and the number of good people seems to shrink each day. It's enough to rattle anyone's nerves and depress even the most optimistic person.

But this shouldn't come as a surprise. Today's verse says that setting your mind on the "flesh" (that is, the things of this world) leads straight to death. But dwelling on spiritual matters leads to life and peace. How? By opening our minds to a greater reality that transcends the ugliness we see all around us. When we look through sin-colored glasses, the violence on the streets becomes louder than the silent working of God's love in the hearts of His children. But when we trade our worldly viewpoint for a spiritual one, we start to glimpse God's master plan cutting like a small but growing stream through the midst of the pain.

This imperfect world is fading fast. . .but God's perfect kingdom will last forever.

PRAYER STARTER:

Lord, help me to see You everywhere I look. Give me spiritual eyes to comprehend that this life isn't the end.

FUTURE INSPIRATION

*I shall not die, but live, and declare
the works of the LORD.*
PSALM 118:17 KJV

. . . .

Sometimes a panic attack comes with the overwhelming feeling that death is near. You feel like you're stepping off a dangerous cliff, and your mind screams, *It's happening!* But you don't seem to fall—you just exist in a sense of emotional fear and dread that subsides only after the attack has run its course.

During these horrifying moments, hold on to today's verse. Know that these attacks don't last forever, nor are they fatal. Remind yourself that everything—even your worst panic attack—happens for a reason. . .and that once it's over, you can declare God's goodness for bringing you through.

This is a strategy not just for panic attacks but for any moment you feel nervous or depressed. Try shifting your thoughts away from the present crisis and toward your future deliverance. Imagine your future self praising God for bringing you through yet another trial, serving as an inspiration for anyone who's experiencing the same.

PRAYER STARTER:

Father, thank You for infusing purpose into my worst moments. Someday I'll die. . .but not today if I still have work to do for You.

HEART DISEASE

Watch over your heart with all diligence,
for from it flow the springs of life.
PROVERBS 4:23 NASB

. . . .

Negativity is like a virus. Consume enough of it, and it will start using your brain as a place to multiply and take control. Depressing, anxious thoughts that once flowed from outside sources—like social media or news sites—soon spread like wildfire, forming deeply ingrained pathways of fear and sadness across your brain. Then, once these pathways are forged, their roots creep down from inside your head, reaching toward the most precious part of you—your heart. Once they've got your heart, it quite literally takes an act of God to set you free.

Don't let things come to that! If you feel burdened by insecurities and fear, try pinpointing a potential cause—the inlet through which negativity is accessing your thoughts. And if cutting yourself off from that source doesn't help, start reaching out to family, friends, and Christian counselors for help in rewiring your mental pathways. As long as you've got the desire to change, the negativity hasn't conquered your heart.

There's still time to kill this virus!

PRAYER STARTER:

God, please help me guard my heart from the
fear and sadness that threaten to take hold.

NOT YET

*Thou hast turned for me my mourning into
dancing: thou hast put off my sackcloth,
and girded me with gladness.*
PSALM 30:11 KJV

. . . .

Today's psalm is a "rearview mirror" prayer. No longer
is the psalmist crying for help in his darkest hour—
he's rejoicing, for his long-awaited deliverance has
finally come. The praise that God has always deserved
finally flows freely from the psalmist's lips, unob-
structed by the fog of fear and deep depression.

Such a place may seem light-years away right
now. . .and that's okay. It's fine, even advisable, to be
honest about your feelings—to admit this happiness
just hasn't arrived yet. But don't miss the important
word there: *yet.* Even your worst moment is little more
than a fading shadow—a painful but brief footnote in
your life's story. For the Christian teen whose hope
rests in God, there's no pain so strong that it lasts
forever. Even if you don't feel Him, God is right beside
you, nudging you forward through this valley. Soon,
you'll find yourself on the mountaintop of joy, where
the pain of today will fade into the haze of the past.

And on that day, you'll find the strength to join the
psalmist in his song.

PRAYER STARTER:

*Thank You, God, for promising a brighter future—
for turning my mourning into dancing.*

A CLOUD OF WITNESSES

Therefore, since we also have such a great cloud of witnesses surrounding us. . .let's run with endurance the race that is set before us.
HEBREWS 12:1 NASB

. . . .

Earlier in this book, we talked about Martin Luther's traumatic struggle with anxiety. But did you know there are countless other Christians throughout history who share the same story?

Ignatius of Loyola, for example, who lived in the fifteenth and sixteenth centuries, suffered from severe obsessive-compulsive disorder. Most people believe Saint Augustine, in the fourth century, had depression, as did the famous Mother Teresa (1910–1997). Author C. S. Lewis (1898–1963) openly described his own struggles in the book *A Grief Observed*, and preacher Charles Spurgeon (1834–1892) spoke of his "shapeless, undefinable, yet, all-beclouding hopelessness."

In short, you're not alone. There's an ever-growing cloud of witnesses that surrounds you—a countless multitude of like-minded Christians who've fought the mist of despair and, through God's help, have won. So don't lose heart! Today's pain may feel all-encompassing, but there's a greater joy that waits just around the corner.

PRAYER STARTER:

God, I thank You for the many faithful Christians who serve as examples for me. Help me to remember that, despite what my mind may say, I'm never alone.

THE CAVE OF DEPRESSION

"The sons of Israel have. . .killed Your prophets with the sword. And I alone am left; and they have sought to take my life."
1 Kings 19:10 NASB

. . . .

Talk about feeling alone. Elijah was one of the strongest men of God in the Bible, yet today's passage finds him in a cave, hiding from Queen Jezebel's murderous rage. Having watched in horror as God's prophets were killed one by one, Elijah assumed that he was next. . .that God had turned His back on His servant.

At that moment, Elijah felt a terrible combination of anxiety and depression—a fear for his life and a profound sadness at being alone. But God didn't leave him in this downcast state; instead, He spoke to Elijah in a still, small voice (19:12), informing him of the existence of seven thousand other men who still remained faithful.

This encouragement was just what Elijah needed. Wiping away his tears, he stood up, took a deep breath, and left the cave as the sun rose over the hills. His darkest hour was over—now, it was time to finish the work God had called him to do.

PRAYER STARTER:

Lord, please meet me in the cave of my depression, offering the encouragement I need to get up and keep going.

WORLDLY GRIEF

*For godly grief produces a repentance
that leads to salvation without regret,
whereas worldly grief produces death.*
2 CORINTHIANS 7:10 ESV

Paul was well acquainted with grief. Blinded on the road
to Damascus, he was stricken with a "godly grief" over
his past sins, thus producing a life-changing repentance. But as implied in a previous chapter (1:8–9),
he also knew the pain of a "worldly grief"—the cold
knife of despair that's often accompanied by the fear
of death. But thankfully, God alleviated Paul's grief by
turning his focus upward and later sending Titus to
encourage him (1:9; 7:6).

If you're a Christian who's trying to live by God's
commands, the grief of regret no longer has a place
in your spiritual development. But the other type of
sadness—worldly grief—is sometimes unavoidable. It
often comes when you least expect it, blindsiding you
with its sheer force. But in these moments of despair,
God will offer a way of escape (1 Corinthians 10:13). It's
up to you, however, to take the brighter path whenever
it becomes apparent.

Are you ready to leave that grief behind?

PRAYER STARTER:

*Thank You, God, for offering hope in the
midst of my depression. Open my eyes
to see the lifeline You're tossing.*

NO JOURNEY TOO LONG

But the angel of the LORD came back a second time and touched him, and said, "Arise, eat; because the journey is too long for you."
1 KINGS 19:7 NASB

. . . .

"God will never give you more than what you can bear." Maybe you've heard this inspiring quote many times. Maybe it sounded great in Sunday school, and perhaps it even gave you encouragement through a series of small trials.

But then the "big one" hit, and you realized just how hollow this saying really is.

God sometimes *does* give you more than you can handle, as shown by today's verse. The journey is often too long and the pain too great for you to bear on your own. If the mountain ahead looks too steep for you to climb, that's probably because it is! But here's the good news: You're not on your own. You don't have to rely on your own strength when God's strength is holding you up. Your darkest hour is when God's power—not your own—is most evident.

Today, don't stop fighting against anxiety and depression. . .but always remember that your victory will ultimately come from God.

PRAYER STARTER:

God, help me to rely on Your power for my deliverance. With You, no journey is too hard for me to handle.

PAINFUL PRAISE

And he said, "Naked I came from my mother's womb, and naked shall I return. The Lord gave, and the Lord has taken away; blessed be the name of the Lord."

JOB 1:21 ESV

Very few people in history have had it worse than Job. Not only was he completely innocent—and undeserving of all the pain and heartbreak he faced—his incredible losses came quickly, one after another. For most of us, life is threaded with beads of sorrow that arrive every few years or so. For Job, the sorrow was concentrated in a bowling ball of grief that crashed down on his head at once.

Still, Job found the strength to bless God. How? By focusing on God's character rather than his own suffering. Job knew that even if he left this world as naked as a newborn baby, it was God who had given him all he had to begin with. No matter what happened, God was still God. He was Job's one point of reference, his anchor in a sea of loss.

Today, don't be afraid to fight your negative feelings with the truth of God's unfailing love.

PRAYER STARTER:

Lord, during my time of suffering, give me the strength to praise Your name.

HANG ON

*The Lord said, "I Myself will go with
you. I will give you rest."*
EXODUS 33:14 NLV

. . . .

Anxiety and depression will try their best to convince
you that following God isn't worth it anymore. Your
emotions will feed your mind with empty promises
of freedom or maybe a resentment toward spiritual
matters. During these times, let today's verse be your
counterattack.

Any Christian who's ever escaped the fires of panic
and loneliness knows how foolish it would've been to
give up on God. Though the temptation was strong at
the time, hindsight is always 20/20. Not a single soul
has ever regretted hanging on to God. . .while many
have regretted letting go. Why? Because, among other
reasons, only God offers true rest. Sure, things like
alcohol and illegal drugs can offer a quick fix, but this
"fix" soon becomes a problem of its own—an even
greater problem, in fact.

Today, when it feels like you need to let go, ask God
for the strength to hang on. As long as you're seeking
His rest, He'll make sure you'll find it.

PRAYER STARTER:

*Father God, I know You'll never let
go of me. . .so please give me the
strength to always hold on to You.*

A BROKEN HEART

*The sacrifice you desire is a broken spirit. You will
not reject a broken and repentant heart, O God.*
PSALM 51:17 NLT

. . . .

When you feel broken. . .when you come before God
with too many thoughts to put into words. . .when
you're fighting back tears—that's when you are closest
to your Creator.

God loves everyone, but He seems to focus His
greatest attention on broken people (Luke 5:32).
There's something about the act of laying your pride
and dignity at God's feet that attracts His undivided
attention. Maybe it's the mere presence of humility that
He loves to see in His children, or perhaps it's the simple
fact that brokenness presents a greater opportunity to
demonstrate His power to heal. Just as Jesus spent His
time healing the sick—and criticizing those who were
unable to see their own brokenness—so He is drawn to
those who come to Him for healing. There's no shame
in admitting your broken heart to God. . .that's exactly
the attitude God is most likely to accept.

PRAYER STARTER:

*Lord Jesus, sometimes I'm a mess. I can't put my
life together on my own—I need You to take my
broken pieces and make from them a masterpiece.*

KNOW THAT HE KNOWS

The Lord knows how to rescue the godly from trials.
2 PETER 2:9 ESV

. . . .

One of fear's primary drivers is the fact that we don't know how the future will play out. Perhaps you see a challenge up ahead—your first job interview, a big test, a speaking presentation, or even a move to a new city—and you're not sure how to face it. Maybe it looms over your thoughts, increasing your anxiety the nearer it gets.

If so, today's verse has some great news: even if you don't know how to get through the trial, God does. He sees everything—even the problems that aren't on your radar—and He's already done all the intricate planning. In God's eyes, your life isn't an obstacle course or series of unfortunate events; rather, it's a checklist of all the ways He plans to show His power through you. Once you realize this truth, the only fear that remains is the irrational variety, which is far easier to treat after you recognize it as such.

God knows how to deliver you from any trial. But do *you* know that He knows?

PRAYER STARTER:

Thank You, God, for making plans to get me through this trial. Remind me that You know, even when I don't.

WORST-CASE SCENARIOS

For to me to live is Christ, and to die is gain.
PHILIPPIANS 1:21 ESV

. . . .

Anxiety has a frustrating tendency to make your mind focus on the worst-case scenario. Even on a sunny day or during a relaxing vacation, your brain may be on high alert, just waiting for something awful to happen. The future feels out of your control. . .as if your good fortune has a dark side that's yet to be revealed.

Well, the Bible promises that for the faithful child of God, there's no such thing as a worst-case scenario. Every outcome not only has a silver lining but becomes the best-case scenario once the bigger picture is considered. Even death is no big deal; in fact, as Paul implied in today's verse, all death does is lead us to an eternity with God.

So today, rather than spend your time fretting over what might happen next, focus on all the ways God might be using your circumstances for good. Chances are your situation isn't life or death. . .but even if it is, know that you're a winner either way.

PRAYER STARTER:

*Thank You, Lord, for making sure
I'm always a winner!*

BURIED TALENTS

"Master, I knew you to be a hard man, reaping where you did not sow, and gathering where you scattered no seed, so I was afraid, and I went and hid your talent in the ground."
MATTHEW 25:24–25 ESV

. . . .

Today's passage is relatable for any Christian teen who feels insecure about the gifts God gives those who love Him.

As you advance toward adulthood, it may be tempting to ignore the growing weight of responsibility. But it may also be tempting to let that weight paralyze you with feelings of inadequacy and fear. *What if I'm not good enough?* you may think. *It's better for me just to slink into the shadows, unnoticed. I'd hate to make a mess of the gifts God has given me.*

But as the master's reply to the servant shows (25:26), the only way you can squander your talents is by *not* using them. God hasn't given you unique abilities so you can impress your friends. He wants you to look past your insecurities and use those gifts to change the world.

How are you using your talents today?

PRAYER STARTER:

God, I don't want to bury my talents— help me to use them for Your glory.

STOP, THIEF!

*"The thief comes only to steal and kill
and destroy; I came so that they would
have life, and have it abundantly."*
JOHN 10:10 NASB

. . . .

It's no secret that anxiety and depression are dirty, rotten thieves. They sneak in uninvited, carrying out the best of your peace and happiness. So Satan loves seeing these emotions in the mind of a Christian teen. After all, they do his best work for him.

Jesus, on the other hand, promises not to steal but to give. His presence is not a vortex but a fountain, filling your soul with the joy the enemy tried to take. When depressing thoughts and anxieties are keeping you awake at night, try focusing on Jesus' love and the promises He makes to those who believe. When depression tells you, *You're not a good person,* tell your depression, *I have Jesus' righteousness!* When anxiety tells you, *You don't have a future,* tell your anxiety, *My future is with God!* When the demons in your mind scream, *Nobody loves you,* whisper back to those demons, *God sent His Son to die for me!*

Today, it's time to shine a spotlight on the thief that works in the shadows. . .then force him to give back what's yours.

PRAYER STARTER:

*Thank You, Jesus, for giving me security
against the cleverest of thieves.*

SUNRISE

Weeping may endure for a night,
but joy cometh in the morning.
PSALM 30:5 KJV

. . . .

Imagine you're hiking in the woods one late autumn evening. Suddenly, you have a terrible realization: you're lost, the sun is setting, and a snowstorm is brewing. What is the first thing you should do? Look for food? No. Your top priority is to find shelter—a place to stay when the cold sets in and the weather takes a turn for the worse.

Chances are you won't get much sleep that night. The relentless chill and perhaps a fear of bears will keep you wide awake, eagerly awaiting the sunrise. When morning dawns and you see the shimmer of light on the horizon, it will feel as if heaven itself has opened above your head.

That's the emotion today's verse describes. A severe bout of depression or anxiety can be a lot like spending a night in the woods—you feel helpless and outmatched by forces beyond your control. But by taking shelter in God's love and promises, you'll find the strength to endure until the sun peeks above the hills.

What a glorious sunrise that will be.

PRAYER STARTER:

Thank You, God, for promising a dawn for every night—a sunrise for every dark sky.

SIDE QUESTS

Let us hear the conclusion of the whole matter:
Fear God, and keep his commandments:
for this is the whole duty of man.
ECCLESIASTES 12:13 KJV

In the game of life, it's so easy to fall into the trap of peer pressure, chasing after the latest stuff, and trying to conform to the world's definition of *cool* or *popular*. Sometimes we get so wrapped up in trying to appease others that our own mental health suffers. We become anxious or depressed, worried that we'll never fit in.

Today's verse, however, reminds us that these worldly pursuits are nothing more than distractions. The true purpose of our lives is not to gain recognition or money—it's to worship God. And as long as we're following the clear path toward this ultimate goal, there's no need for us to venture off the road: we'll automatically find everything we need along the way.

Today, focus yourself on the main objective. Focus on giving God the praise He deserves. . .and trusting Him to provide the blessings we don't.

PRAYER STARTER:

Holy God, thank You for Your unfailing love, mercy, and righteousness. Today, I commit to following Your commands, not becoming distracted by unimportant pleasures.

REFUGE

*He will cover you with his feathers. He will
shelter you with his wings. His faithful
promises are your armor and protection.*
PSALM 91:4 NLT

Today's verse presents two metaphors describing God's protection. The first one compares Him to a protective mother hen who shields her chicks from the rain by hiding them beneath her wings. It's a gentle, reassuring image, designed to comfort the downcast.

The second image, however, offers a jarring shift in tone. No longer is the setting a farmyard on a rainy day—it's a battlefield, complete with the *whiz* of deadly arrows and the relieving *thud* as they bounce off the soldier's shield. This is a much tougher image, designed to give strength to those in the heat of panic or despair.

In other words, today's verse promises that whatever the severity of your inner anguish, one thing remains true: God is your protection. He can be the warm and gentle encourager, and He can be the powerful shield against the most fearsome, damaging enemy. In your darkest moments, you can always turn to Him for refuge.

PRAYER STARTER:

*Father, I need Your protection today.
Shield me from my despairing thoughts
and remind me of Your invincible love.*

LISTENING EAR

Now when John heard in prison about the deeds of the Christ, he sent word by his disciples and said to him, "Are you the one who is to come, or shall we look for another?"
MATTHEW 11:2–3 ESV

Depression can be an unrelenting force in the mind of a Christian teen. If it's left untreated, it can be detrimental to your faith. This isn't just a modern phenomenon—it even dates back to John the Baptist, the original disciple of Jesus.

John had had indisputable evidence of Jesus' divinity, including a voice from heaven that thunderously proclaimed Him as God's Son. But in the cool, damp confines of a prison cell, despair hijacked John's rationality. He began to doubt Jesus' true identity.

So how did Jesus respond to John's lapse of faith? Did He criticize John or call him a bad Christian? No. He simply reminded John of the miracles He'd performed. Jesus understood John's emotional turmoil and gave him just what he needed to press on.

Today, be honest with God about all your thoughts. You'll never work through your doubts and fears by pretending they don't exist.

PRAYER STARTER:

God, thank You for offering an uncritical, listening ear whenever I come to You with questions.

SEEK THEN FIND

Finally, brothers, rejoice. Aim for restoration, comfort one another, agree with one another, live in peace; and the God of love and peace will be with you.
2 CORINTHIANS 13:11 ESV

. . . .

Today's verse offers some golden advice on how to get along with others.

Don't harbor grudges that impact your own emotional state as much as your relationships. Instead, "aim for restoration," trading your thoughts of vengeance for a desire to forgive. Instead of isolating yourself when depression and anxiety strike, "comfort one another," using your shared experiences to offer unique and effective help. Instead of getting involved in pointless and frustrating arguments—in real life or on social media—strive to "agree with one another" and "live in peace" with those who have differing opinions.

If we do all these things, the verse says, "the God of love and peace will be with [us]." In other words, God won't give His peace to someone who's always looking for trouble. To find His peace, you've got to want it first.

For the Christian teen, the search for happiness and contentment starts in the heart.

PRAYER STARTER:

Lord, strengthen my relationships with other people by making me more willing to seek Your peace.

THE DARKEST PATHS

And Job said: "Let the day perish on which I was born, and the night that said, 'A man is conceived.' Let that day be darkness!"
JOB 3:2–4 ESV

Out of context, the words in today's scripture make it seem like Job was going through an emo phase.

Kidding aside, Job's intense anguish becomes much more understandable once you realize his predicament. Not only had his children and all his possessions perished in a string of improbable calamities, his very health was now fading fast. The only consolation Job had left was his wife. . .who was now pressuring him to curse God and die. But as we know, despair was merely a pit stop in Job's story. At the end of the book, we read that God not only restored his blessings but did it twofold (42:10). Job's suffering had been strong, but God's love and mercy proved even stronger.

If you relate to the words in today's scripture, don't worry: Your pain won't last forever. God will make sure you not only escape this anguish but walk out with a stronger resolve to follow Him. As Job's example shows, the darkest paths often wind up in the brightest destinations.

PRAYER STARTER:

Thank You, God, for making sure every trial has an end.

YOUR PAST IS PAST

Then Moses was afraid, and thought, "Surely the thing is known." When Pharaoh heard of it, he sought to kill Moses. But Moses fled from Pharaoh and stayed in the land of Midian.
EXODUS 2:14–15 ESV

. . . .

When you think of Moses, what words come to mind? Strong leader? Noble follower of God? Murderer?

Yes, you read that right. Moses had killed an Egyptian for beating a Hebrew slave, and now he was on the run for his life. This mad sprint to safety eventually led him to the land of Midian, where he stayed as a lowly shepherd for forty long years. He knew his people were suffering, but he was too ashamed of his past even to show his face again. . .at least until God called him to free the Hebrews from bondage.

Chances are you've never done anything to warrant forty years of hiding. But how often do your mistakes weigh heavily on your mind? Today, it's time to come out of the wilderness of self-loathing and step into the light of God's grace. Your past is past—God is calling you now to do something great. Are you ready to join in?

PRAYER STARTER:

Thank You, Jesus, for erasing my sins and giving me hope and purpose for the future.

SAME ACTION, DIFFERENT RESPONSE

And [Peter] went out and wept bitterly. . . .
[Judas] went away and hanged himself.
MATTHEW 26:75; 27:5 NASB

. . . .

What did Peter and Judas have in common? Peter was the man Jesus said would be the rock on which the church would be built (Matthew 16:18). Judas Iscariot owns the most infamous name in history (Matthew 26:14). But they both betrayed their loyalty to Jesus.

So why is Peter revered as one of the most important Christians who ever lived? Why did Jesus entrust the keys of God's kingdom to Peter's preaching? Why didn't Judas get the same chance at redemption?

The truth is he did. But Judas, crumbling under the immense weight of his sin, rejected the forgiveness that could have been his. Instead of repenting, Judas chose to end it all. Peter, however, didn't let his grief destroy him. The next time he met Jesus, his Lord embraced him with open arms. . .and Peter gladly accepted this undeserved forgiveness.

All of us sin, occasionally doing things we believed we'd never do. But we don't have to let our grief swallow us whole. Instead, we can run into Jesus' open arms.

PRAYER STARTER:

Lord, I choose to find a future in Your forgiveness.

DEPRESSED BUT FAITHFUL

For we do not want you to be unaware, brothers and sisters, of our affliction which occurred in Asia, that we were burdened excessively, beyond our strength, so that we despaired even of life.
2 CORINTHIANS 1:8 NASB

• •

Other than Jesus, you'd be hard-pressed to find someone whose faith and determination exceeded Paul's. It seemed Paul was almost superhuman in his spiritual capabilities—as if not even the strongest persecution could upset his soul. But today's verse shatters that illusion. Paul was a giant in the faith, but he was also human like us. He experienced the depths of depression, even to the point of wanting to die, as the verse above implies.

Why would God allow His faithful servant to undergo such a brutal trial? Well, the next verse gives the first reason: "So that we would not trust in ourselves, but in God who raises the dead." Now Paul's suffering serves as an immortal example for Christians who face depression today. Just as Paul's despair eventually ended, replaced by renewed faith and encouragement, so our trials will soon fade into memory, replaced by the knowledge of God's goodness and grace.

PRAYER STARTER:

Thank You, Lord, for Paul's example.
Give me the strength to endure this moment of darkness so I can see Your glorious light.

NO CONDEMNATION

*For God sent not his Son into the world
to condemn the world; but that the world
through him might be saved.*

JOHN 3:17 KJV

. . . .

Depression is a many-headed beast, manifesting in various areas of our lives. Some types of depression require in-depth treatment to cure. . .while others can be resolved simply by gaining a proper understanding of God's love toward us.

If you're a Christian teen struggling with guilt, today's verse is a lifesaver.

How often do you think God is angry with you over something you've done? How often do you refuse to pray out of fear that doing so would only anger Him more? How often do you imagine God as the stereotypical old-man-in-the-sky-with-a-lightning-bolt, ready to punish you for your mistakes?

If that's something you struggle with, know that Jesus' whole mission is to *forgive* repentant sinners, not punish them! He's a doctor, not a tormentor—a friend, not an enemy. If you've asked for forgiveness, there's no need to fear His disapproval or cringe before His judgment. You're one of His sons, and you have a place with Him in eternity.

PRAYER STARTER:

Lord, thank You for loving me more than I love myself.

UNDER YOUR ROOF

You know what I long for, Lord;
you hear my every sigh.
PSALM 38:9 NLT

How amazing is it that the God who created the universe—a vast expanse of billions of stars and galaxies—can still hear your faintest sigh?

When your heart is burdened by life's struggles—whether you've just had a hard day at school or someone you love has died—God cares. He isn't some nebulous force looking down on the cosmos with a vague look of disdain and disapproval. No, He's right beside you, listening to every word and compassionately nodding along as you spill out your thoughts. He's walked this earth just like you do, so He knows from experience how hard life's trials can be. He knows what it feels like to be rejected, anxious, depressed, downcast, and misunderstood. He's a personal God, so He's always there to console you in the midst of your personal problems.

If you feel your prayers are bouncing off the ceiling, rest assured: God is under your roof.

PRAYER STARTER:

Lord Jesus, thank You for paying attention to my
sorrow and pain. Continuously remind me of
Your presence in the midst of deep depression.

CONTRADICTION?

We are full of sorrow and yet we are always happy.
2 CORINTHIANS 6:10 NLV

How can a Christian be "full of sorrow" yet "always happy"? Isn't that a contradiction? On the surface, yes. But when you look at Paul's true meaning, this puzzling statement becomes clear.

Sorrow, as it's defined here, is a state of mind—an emotion you feel based on your situation. Failed that test at school? You're probably feeling a certain degree of sorrow right now. Being made fun of for your faith? It hurts, no doubt about it. Watching as a loved one's health slowly declines? That's one of the worst feelings in the world.

But even in the midst of this mental sorrow, you can have happiness. . .in your soul. Unlike your brain, your soul can look beyond your circumstance—because it's connected directly to God, who works nonstop to bring good from every bad situation. So even when you feel crushed by the weight of sadness and gloom, you can rest in the fact that God is carrying it all.

PRAYER STARTER:

Lord, please give my heart a song when my mind doesn't feel like singing. Thank You for a hope that extends beyond my circumstance.

FUTURE SINS

And lead us not into temptation,
but deliver us from evil.
MATTHEW 6:13 KJV

. . . .

Because we live in a fallen world, sin is always toying with our minds, reminding us of its presence in our lives—and if not in our past then in our future. *What sins might I commit tomorrow?* you may think. *What if I suddenly decide to turn my back on God?*

If you struggle with such fears, let today's verse be your prayer. God won't allow you to be tempted without also offering an escape route (1 Corinthians 10:13), so you don't have to worry about being suddenly trapped in an unavoidable sin. And as for the chance of you rejecting God tomorrow? Well, the very fact that you're concerned about this possibility proves that you're safe in God's care. He's not going to let His children accidentally slip through His fingers! As long as you have the desire to walk with God, He will make sure you have the strength to do it.

Don't let the prospect of sin cloud your future—God is powerful enough to save you from yourself.

PRAYER STARTER:

Thank You, God, for giving me such assurance
about my salvation. Keep leading me
away from the paths of wickedness.

LIMITLESS GRACE

God saved you by his grace when you believed.
And you can't take credit for this; it is a gift from God.
EPHESIANS 2:8 NLT

. . . .

Some people try using this verse to justify sin. *I'm saved by grace*, they think, *so I can do what I want.* Nothing could be further from the truth (Romans 6:1–2)! Rather, this verse serves as a great shield against any faith-related anxieties a Christian might face.

Are you worried that you're just not good enough for God to accept? You're saved by grace. Are you crumbling beneath the weight of your endless efforts to "make things right" with God—to atone for your past sins? You're saved by grace. Are you scared that you might stumble in the future? You're saved by grace.

As long as you're walking with God, there's no need to feel anxiety about your standing in His eyes. Any tension you still feel either stems from an improper understanding of His love or a generalized unease that's perhaps more biological than spiritual. God doesn't leave His kids floundering without answers—He wants nothing more than to reassure you of His limitless grace.

PRAYER STARTER:

Whenever I get nervous about whether I'm right with You, Lord, remind me that Your grace knows no limits.

INVISIBLE ARMIES

So the LORD opened the eyes of the young man, and he saw, and behold, the mountain was full of horses and chariots of fire all around Elisha.
2 KINGS 6:17 ESV

. . . .

Today's verse just has that indescribable *wow* factor. In a moment, Elisha's servant went from shaking in his boots at the Syrian army surrounding him to being amazed by the full power of God. Talk about a spiritual whiplash! All it took was a glimpse of God's work to dissolve the man's fear and snap him back into reality.

Do you ever feel like Elisha's servant? Are the growing responsibilities of adulthood troubling you? Do you feel nervous about being a Christian in this world? If so, let God's Word open your eyes to the power all around you. Read about the miracles He performed for His struggling people. Put yourself in their shoes, imagining what it must have felt like to be delivered from certain death. Then apply these truths to your own life. Consciously replace your fear with the faith that God is surrounding you with protection today.

PRAYER STARTER:

Thank You, God, for offering these eye-opening glimpses of Your might. When the armies of fear surround me, remind me that You've got armies of Your own.

SAVED!

Say to those with anxious heart, "Take courage, fear not. Behold, your God will come with vengeance; the retribution of God will come, but He will save you."
ISAIAH 35:4 NASB

. . . .

Today's verse is a double-sided sword. On one side, there's a stern warning for anyone who walks in disobedience to God: His wrath is coming. When that day comes, you do *not* want to be on His bad side. But on the other hand, this verse offers a great hope for God's followers. As fire rains down all around us, we Christians will be saved by His everlasting grace—not because we were good but because we trusted in a good Lord.

So how does that relate to the stress and sadness we experience today? By being assured of our eternal life to come, we don't have to worry about the trials that come in this life. Sure, as long as we're on this earth we'll still feel the emotions of shock, disgust, nervousness, and loneliness—but we don't have to let those feelings seep into our soul. Because we're right with God, we can "take courage" and "fear not." His love has saved us from death!

PRAYER STARTER:

Lord, thank You for saving me from the punishment my sin deserves. Remind me of this freedom every time I start feeling hopeless.

ANXIOUS THOUGHTS

Search me, God, and know my heart; put me
to the test and know my anxious thoughts.
PSALM 139:23 NASB

. . . .

In the verses leading up to today's scripture, the psalmist gives voice to his rather extreme thoughts about the violent, hateful men who surround him. Statements like "Put the wicked to death, God" and "I hate them" (139:19, 22) don't seem very Christlike, do they?

But that's the point. This psalm's purpose is to show us that no thought, no matter how extreme, can be hidden from God. . .so we might as well tell Him what we're thinking. There's no use in trying to hide our bitterness, resentment, fear, anxiety, regret, or darkest desire from the Lord who knows all these things in the first place. That's why the psalmist says, "Search me, God," and in the next verse, "See if there is any hurtful way in me, and lead me in the everlasting way" (139:24 NASB).

Letting these thoughts fester inside will only amplify their power. But telling them to someone who will listen with a compassionate, nonjudgmental ear—in this case, God—will not only provide relief but set you on the path toward healthier emotions.

PRAYER STARTER:

God, search me for thoughts that don't
honor You. Help me to deal with them
before they start dealing with me.

ANTIDOTE

*When my anxious thoughts multiply within
me, Your comfort delights my soul.*
PSALM 94:19 NASB

• •

Anxiety can work like a disease, infecting the brain with
a seemingly trivial concern that soon mushrooms into
monstrous proportions. But today's verse expresses
this idea even more clearly, conjuring images of a deadly
virus that multiplies within the mind.

But if anxiety is a virus, that begs the question:
What's the antidote?

There may be times you'll need to seek profes-
sional treatment for persistent, irrational fears. But
up to and including those times, God's Word can offer
comforting answers to your most distressing questions.
It is medicine for the troubled mind—the antidote for
uncertainty. When your brain is screaming, the still,
small voice of God's Word can drown it out. When your
heart feels like it's about to explode, biblical promises
can steady its rhythm. When you just *know* something
bad is about to happen, you can turn to something else
you know: the assurance of eternal life and a God who
loves you no matter what.

Today, let God's comfort be the cure for your
disease.

PRAYER STARTER:

*Lord, whenever my anxiety starts growing,
remind me of my status as Your child.
Be the antidote to the sickness within.*

SPIRITUAL SEALANT

*"Do not let your heart be troubled. You have put
your trust in God, put your trust in Me also."*
JOHN 14:1 NLV

. . . .

Jesus' disciples must have been shocked. Not only had
their Master just promised that one of them would
betray Him (John 13:21), He went on to strongly imply
His death at the hands of the government (13:33). And
what did He say after these life-changing revelations?
"Do not let your heart be troubled."

Okay, Jesus. . .easier said than done.

Of course, Jesus knew His disciples would feel fear—
He Himself felt that emotion as He prayed in the garden
(Luke 22:44). So His command wasn't for the disciples to
walk around like unfeeling robots. No, He wanted them
to avoid letting this fear seep into their hearts. Like a
plank of waterproofed wood that gets wet in the rain
but never absorbs the moisture, we can travel through
a period of loneliness and distress without assimilating
these emotions into our character. How? By applying
Jesus' promises—the best spiritual sealant for our souls.

PRAYER STARTER:

*Thank You, Jesus, for fear-proofing my
soul. Even when I'm afraid, I know Your
love is strong enough to bring me out.*

MINOR PERSECUTIONS

But even if you should suffer for
righteousness' sake, you will be blessed.
Have no fear of them, nor be troubled.
1 PETER 3:14 ESV

. . . .

Are you afraid of persecution? When you're in public—at
school, with your friends, or even walking down the
street—do you ever try to downplay your faith? Are you
worried that your devotion to Jesus will earn the ire of
some of your friends? If so, maybe it's time to consider
the context behind today's verse.

When Peter wrote this letter, Rome's persecution
of Christians was just beginning. Over the next few
decades, believers would regularly face torture, crucifixion, immolation, or, occasionally, a cruel blend of
all of these. Yet Peter told his readers, "Have no fear
of them, nor be troubled." What would Peter say to us
modern Christians, whose worst fear involves getting
a dirty look or being unfriended on social media?

Today, spend some time dwelling on the early
Christians' sacrifice. . .and use their unbroken dedication as fuel for your own. Just as God welcomed these
godly men and women home with open arms, so too
He'll reward you if you only stay the course.

PRAYER STARTER:

Lord, please don't let minor persecutions
get to me. Remind me of the great reward
that awaits me in heaven with You.

SLIP AND SLIDE

*Give your burdens to the LORD, and he will take care
of you. He will not permit the godly to slip and fall.*
PSALM 55:22 NLT

· ·

Depending on your fear of heights, you'll see something
truly horrifying on the seventieth floor of the US Bank
Tower in Los Angeles, California. A transparent glass
slide, known as the Skyslide, wraps around the outside
of the building, slinking down to the sixty-ninth floor. At
nearly one thousand feet from the ground, it's one of
the craziest rides in the world. (In case you're sweating
right now, know that it's been permanently closed.)

Anxiety is like the mental version of Skyslide. . .
without any of the fun. When you're having a panic
attack, it feels like the bottom of your life has given
way, suspending you in perpetual free fall. But don't
worry: If you're a Christian, this anxiety is just a glass
slide. No matter what feelings of helplessness and
despair are rushing through your mind, God is holding
you up, preventing you from falling. Even better is the
fact that God's grace is *much* stronger than any piece
of polished glass.

You may not enjoy this ride, but rest assured: it'll
be over before you know it.

PRAYER STARTER:

*Father, thank You for holding me up
when my fear tells me I'm falling.*

INFLEXIBLE

Many plans are in a person's heart,
but the advice of the LORD will stand.
PROVERBS 19:21 NASB

· ·

Are you an overplanner? Do you start to feel nervous when life throws even the mildest of curveballs? If so, today's verse is for you.

Don't misunderstand—planning is a great skill that God gives. It's useful for solving problems and anticipating our response to a tricky situation. But there's just one problem: Planning is unreliable. Sometimes, our plans work; other times, they do not. We might think our plans are foolproof, but God's plans always expose the flaws in our thinking. Is that sometimes unpleasant? Yes. Should we keep chasing our own plans after God reveals His own? No.

If you tend to be inflexible, try doing something spontaneous. Plan your day. . .then look for tiny ways to break your plan. Sticking to your own program might seem less stressful, but in the end, holding on too tightly only leads to frustration.

Don't be a victim of your own inflexibility. Find freedom in God's plans.

PRAYER STARTER:

Lord, give me the wisdom to know Your plan and the courage to follow through with it. Relieve my fear of change—it's the only way I can make a difference.

RAINY DAYS

For everything there is a season, and a time for every matter under heaven. . .a time to weep, and a time to laugh; a time to mourn, and a time to dance.
ECCLESIASTES 3:1, 4 ESV

If you're like most people, you probably prefer warm, sunny days over cold, rainy ones. But as you know, rain is very important to our survival. Without it, wells and rivers would dry up, and we'd face far bigger problems than a ruined picnic.

Similarly, every sad thing that happens in your life, even if you don't see the purpose for it, occurs for a reason. God's not up in the sky placing bets on what disaster befalls you today—He's carefully shielding you from any unnecessary heartbreaks while allowing the ones He knows will benefit you and advance His kingdom. It's okay to vent your frustration during these times—that's what a sizable portion of Psalms is all about. But we must remember that even in the slog of despair, God is reaching out His hand to pull us toward the other side.

PRAYER STARTER:

God, give me a bigger perspective on the bad things that happen to me. Teach me to roll with the punches, knowing that You have a purpose for it all.

PEACE AND RELAXATION

In peace I will both lie down and sleep,
for You alone, LORD, have me dwell in safety.
PSALM 4:8 NASB

- -

Ever have sleepless nights? Does anxiety take advantage of times when you close your eyes, filling your mind with regrets about yesterday and worries about tomorrow? Does your fear work overtime to keep you awake?

If so, today's verse offers some great news: God's promises are an antidote to anxiety-induced insomnia. When all the things that might go wrong tomorrow start surging through your mind, dwell on all the ways God can make them go right. When you start obsessing over what you might have done wrong today, dwell on God's grace that covers your mistakes. When you start wondering if God is even there, dwell on His promise to never leave you.

Tonight, don't lose sleep over things that God has told us not to worry about. When your mind is restless, let God's Word be your source of peace.

PRAYER STARTER:

Please help me to get a solid night's sleep, Lord.
Comfort me with Your promises and remind me of
all the blessings You've already poured into my life.

FACE THE MUSIC

He will rejoice over thee with joy; he will rest in
his love, he will joy over thee with singing.
ZEPHANIAH 3:17 KJV

. . . .

It's a proven fact that music can alleviate stress and relax the troubled soul. But did you know that God Himself is making melody over you?

That's right: the most relaxing song of all comes from the lips of the Lord, who offers us perfect peace and satisfaction. When we're drowning in a sea of self-loathing, we can switch the tune to John 3:16—"For God so loved the world. . ." When we're worried about our future, we can turn our ear to the song of Jeremiah 29:11 (KJV), listening for the "thoughts of peace" that God has toward us. When we feel all alone, we can sway to the rhythm of "I will never desert you" (Hebrews 13:5 NASB).

God's music is the best kind, offering a note of hopefulness that rings true in the middle of life's disharmony. His song leads you to the fulfillment of His amazing promises.

PRAYER STARTER:

God, when the song in my mind is warped and grating, bring me back in tune with Yours.

CLEAR INSTRUCTIONS

"In My Father's house are many rooms; if that were not so, I would have told you, because I am going there to prepare a place for you. And if I go and prepare a place for you, I am coming again and will take you to Myself, so that where I am, there you also will be. And you know the way where I am going."
JOHN 14:2–4 NASB

. . . .

We've all relied on a map or phone to lead us to some new location. If the instructions say, "Turn right," what do you do? Keep going straight because you're not sure where you are? No, you turn right, trusting that the instructions are correct.

Today's scripture is useful for those times when you feel lost, like you're stumbling through life without rhyme or reason. You hear God's voice and you read His instructions, but you have no idea where you are or what move to take next. But that's okay. Why? Because you know where your journey will end—in your heavenly Father's house.

There's no need to question the directions, because God Himself made the map.

PRAYER STARTER:

Lord Jesus, thank You for leaving behind clear instructions on how to get to You.

PERPLEXED

*We are pressed on every side by
troubles, but we are not crushed. We are
perplexed, but not driven to despair.*
2 CORINTHIANS 4:8 NLT

. . . .

If the apostle Paul were to travel to modern times and hear the easygoing, health-and-wealth gospel that many Christians believe, what do you think he'd say? Well, knowing Paul, he'd probably write a whole letter in response. . .with today's verse being the thesis.

You'd be hard-pressed to find examples of Christians who led healthy, wealthy, problem-free lives. Most heroes of the faith lived in constant danger, and many of them even died for their beliefs. Why? Because the Christian life doesn't promise to make your body comfortable—it promises to provide peace for your soul. Paul lived one of the roughest lives in history, yet his spiritual life stayed intact because of his trust in God. He openly admitted that he sometimes became perplexed, but he also bragged about the divine peace that God had given him.

Being a Christian might not make you rich. . .but who needs riches when you have God, the greatest treasure of all?

PRAYER STARTER:

*Lord, remind me of the eternal hope
that Your salvation offers.*

EXTERNAL REALITY

Then Christ will make his home in your hearts
as you trust in him. Your roots will grow down
into God's love and keep you strong.
EPHESIANS 3:17 NLT

. . . .

Our minds have a nasty way of playing tricks on us. Case in point: Have you ever seen a dark shadow in the middle of the night and imagined an intruder crouching at your door? Then you turn on the lamp and see it's just your coat hanging from the knob. When your brain lies to you, you use an external reality—in this case, the light—to expose the truth.

God's Word works like that. When anxiety and depression start lying to you, filling your mind with thoughts of fear, it's time to switch on the light by reminding yourself of God's promises. Jesus' presence in your heart and the scriptures you've memorized will be the chain that keeps you tethered to the facts—your much-needed external reality.

Let God expose your fears for the flimsy lies they really are.

PRAYER STARTER:

God, thank You for calming my heart
when my mind becomes unruly.

PUBLIC SPEAKING

"But when they hand you over, do not worry about how or what you are to say; for what you are to say will be given you in that hour."
MATTHEW 10:19 NASB

. . . .

Out of all the phobias, one fear is consistently ranked at the top: *glossophobia*—the fear of public speaking. And for many Christians, the fear is amplified when this "speaking" involves sharing their faith.

But today's verse says God will help you overcome this debilitating phobia. While you should definitely always be "ready to make a defense to everyone who asks you to give an account for the hope that is in you" (1 Peter 3:15 NASB), you should also resist the urge to fret over the details. That way, when you're put on the spot—when that guy at school suddenly asks you why you go to church—your reply won't be some quivering robotic script but rather a heartfelt response that reveals who you truly are in Christ.

PRAYER STARTER:

Father, help me work past my fear of public speaking, especially when it comes to speaking about You. Give me the words to say, right when I need to say them.

JUNGLE PATH

In all your ways acknowledge Him,
and He will make your paths straight.
PROVERBS 3:6 NASB

. . . .

Without a goal in life, our daily existence can seem like we're meandering through the jungle, looking for a route that isn't there. All our hacking and slashing at the foliage in our way is useless if we don't know which way we're going. It's easy for depression and fatigue to set in as we find ourselves walking in circles, trapped by our repetitive routines.

To make progress, we need a path. And today's verse says that God not only offers such a path but promises to make the path straight. No longer do we have to wander aimlessly through life, searching for what people often call "meaning." Instead, if we acknowledge God and strive to live by His commands, we'll be filled with a fiery motivation to change the world.

This life is a jungle, and there's only one reliable path that can take you to the other side. Have you found that path?

PRAYER STARTER:

Thank You, Lord, for providing me with a motivation—a clear path through a confusing world. Help me to stay on this path today.

IT'S A TRAP!

*The fear of man brings a snare, but one
who trusts in the LORD will be protected.*
PROVERBS 29:25 NASB

. . . .

Have you ever played with a Chinese finger trap? If so, you know how it works: you stick your index fingers in each end of a tiny elastic tube, and then you try pulling them out. . .but the more you try, the tighter the tube's grip becomes.

Well, the fear of other people is just like a Chinese finger trap. The more you try to appease the masses by hiding your identity in Christ, the stronger their grip on you becomes. Pretty soon, you'll live in constant fear that someone might find out your "dirty secret"—your faith in Jesus. In order to preserve what you see as your dignity, you throw away the one part of you that shines the brightest. Fear turns to paranoia, which then turns to bitterness and resentment toward God.

Don't fall into the trap of hiding your light—let it shine before everyone!

PRAYER STARTER:

*Father, help me to be courageous in my desire
to show Your love to others. Replace my fears
and insecurities with a solid trust in You.*

DAILY BREAD

"Give us this day our daily bread."
MATTHEW 6:11 NASB

. . . .

Anxiety is a cruel taskmaster, always expecting more out of you than you can give. Your future, for instance—how much of it do you think you can control? Up to a year? A month? A week? Anxiety would have you believe that if you just think hard enough about it, your future will somehow improve. But If you don't. . .watch out!

This attitude is foolish, of course, but anxiety can turn even the most foolish, logically absurd statements into seemingly airtight arguments. That's why Jesus' words today are so poignant for anyone suffering from panic attacks. Your future, He says, is controlled not by your mind but by God. In fact, you can't even control *tomorrow*, so why stress over what happens a year from now? Day by day, God provides our bread—both our literal nourishment and clothing and shelter and our more abstract needs like being loved.

Yes, anxiety is a cruel taskmaster, but Jesus can free us from its irrational demands. Allow Him to do that in your life.

PRAYER STARTER:

Lord Jesus, thank You for Your day-to-day provision. I know I can't control my future—so I'm trusting Your wisdom and protection instead.

SATISFACTION

Keep your lives free from the love of money.
Be happy with what you have. God has said,
"I will never leave you or let you be alone."
HEBREWS 13:5 NLV

. . . .

Maybe you're not quite old enough to know just how tempting—and devastating—the "love of money" can be. So let's replace the word *money* with something that all teen boys understand: *popularity*, *technology*, *girls*, *likes and follows*, whatever. Any pleasure that threatens to consume your passions and drive you from God is encompassed by the word *money*.

Such obsessions are harmful not only to your spiritual well-being but to your mental health as well. Forever chasing after something that simply cannot satisfy is a surefire method of driving yourself to the brink of insanity. Anxiety and depression set in as your search for meaning grows increasingly desperate...and the results grow increasingly disappointing.

All this can be avoided by putting your trust in the one thing that gives true purpose: God's love. All other pursuits in this life will fade to obscurity and leave you wanting, but God's never-ending love will give you the satisfaction you've always craved.

PRAYER STARTER:

Lord Jesus, help me to find my identity in
You, not in some temporary pleasure that
will only cause me pain in the long run.

THE HERE AND NOW

God is our refuge and strength,
a very present help in trouble.
PSALM 46:1 KJV

. . . .

One good way to combat anxiety and depression is to reflect on the blessings God has provided in the past. But let's face it: sometimes, panic attacks or depressive episodes can be so severe that all memories of the past are either erased or tainted by your current pain. Looking to the past becomes impossible: all that exists is what you're feeling right now.

But today's verse offers hope even in the midst of such storms. It promises that God is much more than a kind mentor who occasionally helps us along the way—He's always right there for you, even in your present suffering. Even when you can't feel Him, His presence is there, giving you the strength to press on. You don't have to think about the past or the future—just dwell on the God who's with you in the here and now. No matter how low you sink, your refuge and strength is simply a prayer away.

PRAYER STARTER:

God, I need You now! I can't always feel Your presence,
but I know You're here. Please give me the strength
to weather this darkness until the morning comes.

WORMS

Fear not, you worm Jacob, you men of Israel!
I am the one who helps you, declares the LORD;
your Redeemer is the Holy One of Israel.
ISAIAH 41:14 ESV

. . . .

Today's verse sounds kind of harsh, doesn't it? Why did God think calling the Israelites a "worm" would help them overcome their fear? Because in order to look past their anxieties about the future, the Israelites needed to give up their sense of self-importance.

Today's culture encourages self-exultation as a form of therapy. And while positive affirmations might help someone who struggles with self-loathing or intense regret, it can also lead to a misplaced sense of pride. Boasting of your own abilities will only increase the expectations you place on yourself. It's far better to consider your helplessness in light of God's power.

On our own, we're all worms, crawling through the dirt of our own ungodly desires. But, thankfully, God hasn't left us on our own—He's given us a divine purpose and endowed us with His Spirit. Recognizing this fact isn't a personal boast—it's a boast on the goodness of God. And *that's* something we should brag about!

PRAYER STARTER:

Thank You, Jesus, for giving me a value
that lies outside my own frail abilities.
Help me to find true confidence in You.

GOD'S GOOD PLEASURE

Fear not, little flock; for it is your Father's
good pleasure to give you the kingdom.
LUKE 12:32 KJV

. . . .

Whenever you make a mistake, do you imagine God
scowling in heaven? Maybe He's just waiting for you
to mess up one more time so He can strike you down
for good. . . . Many Christians have this view of God,
and it's not hard to see why such a misunderstanding
could lead to crippling anxiety and depression.

But there's good news: Today's scripture puts
those fears to rest. God is not waiting for an excuse
to shut you out of His kingdom. No—He's continually
looking for ways to draw you closer to Him. He's not
betting on your failure; He's working to make sure you
reach home.

Don't live in fear of God. Don't run from Jesus,
who died to secure your salvation. Use His promise in
today's verse to fight anxiety's lies and replace them
with the truth of God's Word.

PRAYER STARTER:

God, may I never be afraid of Your forgiveness.
I know that no matter how badly I've messed up,
it's still Your good pleasure to give me the kingdom.

FEAR-CRUSHING POWER

"Look, I have given you authority over all the power of the enemy, and you can walk among snakes and scorpions and crush them. Nothing will injure you."
LUKE 10:19 NLT

. . . .

Before you go walking barefoot through the woods, consider that maybe today's verse isn't discussing literal snakes and scorpions. Jesus described something far more harmful—the enemies of your soul.

Insecurities, worldly lusts, peer pressure, unbridled anxiety, and many other forces can work overtime to pull a Christian teen down, making him feel helpless in the face of such overwhelming evil. The world's a jungle of sin, depression, and dissatisfaction. . .but Jesus promises that His faithful children are immune to the venom of these poisonous creatures. Not only can we walk among them without fear, we can actually crush them beneath the truth of God's Word. We don't have the strength or authority on our own—but Jesus gives us that power through His Spirit.

With a power like that on our side, how can we be afraid?

PRAYER STARTER:

Thank You, Jesus, for giving me a power that crushes all fear.

CREATURE IN THE CLOSET

Therefore if any man be in Christ, he is a
new creature: old things are passed away;
behold, all things are become new.
2 CORINTHIANS 5:17 KJV

. . . .

Many Christian guys treat their past lives—their old "creature"—like a closet buddy, cracking open the door every now and then to reminisce about old times. But when darkness falls in the evening, that creature lets itself out, frightening guys with its monstrous presence.

How can we rid ourselves of such fears? Get rid of the creature. If you're a Christian, your past life cannot be revisited from time to time—it's dead and gone. That creature you're talking to? It's nothing but a skeleton by now—a useless, filthy heap that should be dragged out and tossed in the dumpster. Once you've finished cleaning, you can fill the extra closet space with something far more useful: the full armor of God (Ephesians 6:11–17).

PRAYER STARTER:

Thank You, Lord, for giving me a reason not
to fear the old creature that used to be me.
Help me to dispose of it once and for all.

GHOST STORIES

When the disciples saw Him walking on the sea, they were terrified, and said, "It is a ghost!" And they cried out in fear.
MATTHEW 14:26 NASB

. . . .

Many teenagers like ghost stories. They enjoy the safe but exhilarating rush of adrenaline that scary books and movies provide.

There's just one problem, though: Anxiety has a way of taking this usually harmless fear and applying it to *everything*. You become the protagonist of your own horror flick, tormented by the spirits of uncontrollable thoughts, terrified to look around the corner.

That's the situation in which the disciples found themselves in today's verse. Already spooked by a raging storm and thus expecting the worst, they irrationally concluded that Jesus was an evil spirit bent on their destruction. Rather than embracing their source of rescue, they "cried out in fear" as He approached.

Did that stop Jesus? Of course not! He exclaimed, "Take courage, it is I; do not be afraid" (14:27 NASB). His presence, frightening at first, was just what the disciples needed to be able to conquer their fear.

PRAYER STARTER:

Thank You, Jesus, for easing my mind when I'm afraid. The only ghost that haunts me now is the Holy Ghost—and as long as He's here, I've got nothing to worry about.

ETERNAL LIFE

*But you, beloved, building yourselves up in your
most holy faith and praying in the Holy Spirit, keep
yourselves in the love of God, waiting for the mercy
of our Lord Jesus Christ that leads to eternal life.*
JUDE 20–21 ESV

The book of Jude might just contain the most severe
imagery in the New Testament. Jude describes the
depths of sin and the finality of God's wrath with dis-
turbing detail, and his "fire and brimstone" message
continues throughout most of the short letter. It's
enough to make any sensible non-Christian sweat.

But if you're a Christian, today's passage comes as
a profound reassurance. All this doom and destruction
no longer applies to you—God has, quite literally, pulled
you from the fire and given you eternal life. Even your
worst anxieties and fears have no power over your
soul—they're just minor annoyances, waiting to be
swatted away forever.

Today, hang on to the love of God and let go of
your doubts and fears. No emotion is strong enough
to threaten your relationship with Him.

PRAYER STARTER:

*Lord God, help me to focus on peace and eternal life
whenever my thoughts turn toward fear or death.*

MAKE YOUR JOY COMPLETE

*Though I have many things to write to you,
I do not want to do so with paper and ink;
but I hope to come to you and speak face to
face, so that your joy may be made complete.*
2 JOHN 12 NASB

As social media dawned, people were excited about its seemingly limitless potential. No longer would you lose touch with your friends from high school—you can chat with them from across the world! No longer would social anxiety prohibit people from making friends—anyone can have thousands of friends by just tapping a screen!

While social media has certainly had its benefits, it's also destructive to many teens' mental health. Texting is great, but it just can't replace face-to-face human interaction. Still, many teens act like it can, so feelings of isolation and depression are running rampant.

The apostle John understood this truth, as do practically all modern researchers. So today, if you're struggling with an isolation-fueled depression, turn off your phone and step outside. Find someone to talk to. It might be good for both of you.

PRAYER STARTER:

*Father, help me to build healthy relationships
in real life, not just online. Help me to find ways
to make my (and others') joy complete.*

HIGH EXPECTATIONS

*It is my eager expectation and hope that I
will not be at all ashamed, but that with full
courage now as always Christ will be honored
in my body, whether by life or by death.*
PHILIPPIANS 1:20 ESV

. . . .

For many teens, a common source of anxiety is high
expectations—from their friends, from their families,
and even from themselves. When you feel as if everyone
is counting on you to perform just the way they want
you to, the resulting pressure can be stressful, possibly overwhelming. Even the most flexible substance
on earth, after all, can break under the right amount
of pressure.

Today's verse tells us to have high expectations. . .just not in ourselves. When we're walking in
God's will, we can trust *Him* to provide the strength to
live the way He wants. We know we can't do it alone—
only He has the power to lead us into a holy life. So
we put all our expectations on God, who's more than
willing to bear the pressure.

God will never disappoint your expectations.

PRAYER STARTER:

*Thank You, Jesus, for allowing me to shift my high
expectations off myself and onto Your power.*

HOPE DEFERRED

Hope deferred makes the heart sick,
but a desire fulfilled is a tree of life.
PROVERBS 13:12 ESV

. . . .

Every day of our lives consists of a series of hopes, both small and large. Right now, as you read this sentence, you're probably hoping for a multitude of things subconsciously—that today's devotion will be helpful, that your next meal will be good, that tomorrow's experience won't be terrible, that your planned conversation with that girl goes well, that you can meet up with your friends this weekend.

Of course, not every hope pans out the way we want. . .which is why it's important to have a constant, unchanging hope that never fails. Even if you flunk the test, your dinner tastes awful, and your movie night gets canceled, you'll still have one hope to cling to: eternal life with God. And as long as you have this big hope, sadness over the smaller disappointments suddenly becomes easier to overcome.

PRAYER STARTER:

God, thank You for giving me a hope that
transcends all the petty disappointments
that happen each day. Help me focus on what
matters and overlook the things that don't.

DISASTER

"And there will be signs in sun and moon and stars, and on the earth distress of nations in perplexity because of the roaring of the sea and the waves, people fainting with fear and with foreboding of what is coming on the world. . . . Now when these things begin to take place, straighten up and raise your heads, because your redemption is drawing near."
LUKE 21:25–26, 28 ESV

Different people have different interpretations of the trials today's passage speaks of. But whatever your opinions about end-times theology, we can all agree on one fact: Jesus wants us to place our hope beyond this world.

When you see nations at war with each other, when earthquakes and hurricanes and terrorist attacks threaten your safety—don't think for a moment God has abandoned you. Rather, remember that these catastrophes are just painful reminders that your hope lies not in this life but in the life to come. They're little more than nightmares, ready to vanish forever with the breaking of day.

Depression and anxiety are natural responses to life's calamities. . .but thank God we serve a *super-*natural Savior!

PRAYER STARTER:

Lord Jesus, help me to look beyond the world's sorry state and toward Your eternal kingdom that will one day make all pain and worry obsolete.

UNCHANGING LOVE

Remember my affliction and my wanderings, the wormwood and the gall! My soul continually remembers it and is bowed down within me. But this I call to mind, and therefore I have hope: The steadfast love of the LORD never ceases; his mercies never come to an end.
LAMENTATIONS 3:19–22 ESV

Judging by today's passage (and even the very title of the book it belongs to), it's safe to say the author suffered from severe depression. And why wouldn't he? Jerusalem—God's chosen city—had been destroyed, its inhabitants carried off by the ruthless Babylonians.

But even in the face of such distressing circumstances, the author was able to find comfort. How? By remembering the "steadfast love of the LORD" and His mercies that "never come to an end." Even if all our outward blessings are violently stripped away, we can trust in God to preserve the one thing that matters most: our souls. In the midst of our nervous thoughts and intense grief, we can anchor our peace in His unchanging love.

PRAYER STARTER:

Lord, comfort me in times of loss and deep sadness. Remind me of the eternal joy that awaits at the end of my road.

ICD

*My flesh and my heart faileth: but God is the
strength of my heart, and my portion for ever.*
PSALM 73:26 KJV

. . . .

Heart failure is one of the most dangerous medical
conditions. As you know, your heart is responsible
for pumping life-giving blood to your body. . .so if
it fails, you'll die quickly. As a result, many a person
with heart problems has an "Implantable Cardioverter
Defibrillators" (ICD) installed in their chest. The ICD is
a small device that connects to the heart. If the heart
starts to fail, the ICD sends out a shock to keep the
rhythm intact.

Today's verse compares anxiety and depression
to a bad case of heart failure. . .but also tells us that
God is our ICD. When we have His Word inside us, it
gives our hearts a much-needed boost whenever they
start to fail. How? By reminding us of a love that far
outweighs even the heaviest of sorrows.

God's promises can save your life.

PRAYER STARTER:

*Almighty Lord, my heart is broken and
barely alive. I need Your peace to mend
it and restore my soul to health.*

UNFAIR

*Also, David was in great distress because
the people spoke of stoning him, for all
the people were embittered, each one because
of his sons and his daughters. But David
felt strengthened in the Lord his God.*
1 Samuel 30:6 NASB

. . . .

Have you ever felt like David in today's scripture—like
the whole world is out to get you and you don't know
why? Maybe your friends have turned their backs on
you because of your faith. Maybe all your efforts seem
to come to nothing. Maybe the deck seems stacked
against you, and you're left wondering, *What did I do
to deserve this?*

If so, let David's response be your example. Instead
of dwelling on your bad luck and the resulting resentment, strengthen yourself in the Lord your God. Open
your Bible and erase your frustration with the one
promise that will never disappoint you: the promise
of God's grace.

It's no secret that life is hard and confusing sometimes. But God makes it clear that no matter what
happens, He's still on your side. Don't put off your
cheerfulness until things turn around for the better—
you've got the best treasure in the universe right now.

PRAYER STARTER:

*God, thank You for providing a way for
encouragement to enter my life. Help me to take
advantage of Your peace every chance I get.*

MARK OF PRESERVATION

*And the LORD put a mark on Cain, lest any
who found him should attack him.*
GENESIS 4:15 ESV

. . . .

Cain, the first murderer in history, is the last person you'd expect to receive God's promise of protection. . .but that's exactly what happened. Even though God banished Cain for killing his brother, He also ensured his safety by placing a mysterious mark on his skin. This mark let everyone know, "Don't mess with Cain. . .or else!"

If God can protect a man who murdered his own brother, how much more willing would He be to protect His own children? When you became a Christian, God placed a mark on your soul, letting all the demons in hell know not to mess with you. They can scream and whisper their lies in your ear all they want, but they're simply not permitted to touch your soul. So when the voices of doubt and temptation and fear about your standing with God come knocking, remind these voices of how powerless they truly are.

PRAYER STARTER:

*Lord, thank You for the mark of preservation You've
placed on my soul. May Your promise of an eternal
future help me overcome any fears of tomorrow.*

PATIENCE IS A VIRTUE

*And thus Abraham, having patiently
waited, obtained the promise.*
HEBREWS 6:15 ESV

You probably know this by now, but impatience breeds anxiety. If you're waiting impatiently in a long line at lunch, for instance, every moment of delay will drive you up a wall. And the more impatient you get, the longer each second seems to grow. So what's the best way to handle this situation? By simply trusting that your time will eventually come and shifting your focus to something else. Start a conversation. Think about a story you've read. Do *something* other than obsessing over that silly lunch line.

When it comes to larger struggles, the same strategy applies. Just as Abraham waited patiently—by trusting that God's promise would ultimately come true—so too you can wait on God's timing when life doesn't seem to be going your way. If you're a child of God, everything happens at the right place and time—all you have to do is wait your turn.

PRAYER STARTER:

*Lord, please replace my impatience with a steady
trust in Your promises. I know that no matter
how many setbacks I face, my life is always
marching onward toward an everlasting peace.*

HOPE IN THE DUNGEON

"As for you, you meant evil against me, but God meant it for good in order to bring about this present result, to keep many people alive."
GENESIS 50:20 NASB

. . . .

Put yourself in Joseph's shoes for a moment. You've been sold into slavery by your own brothers, hauled off to Egypt, accused of attempted assault by your new master's wife, thrown into prison, and kept in a dirty dungeon for years—all because you had a dream.

If anyone had a right to be depressed, it'd be Joseph. Yet by trusting in the truth behind today's verse—which came from his own lips after his circumstances turned around—Joseph managed to keep both his faith and his sanity intact.

Today, start fighting back against depression by focusing not on where you are right now but on where God has said that you'll be. Dwell not on the present pain but on God's eternal promise to give meaning to it all. Even the worst thing the world throws at you— sickness, mental illness, the loss of a loved one—will be redeemed once you see how it all fits into God's master plan.

PRAYER STARTER:

Thank You, God, for giving me the example of Joseph. Preserve my faith in You, even when I'm in the dungeon.

FATAL ALLURE

Wine is a mocker, strong drink is raging:
and whosoever is deceived thereby is not wise.
PROVERBS 20:1 KJV

. . . .

The Bible is full of ways to treat anxiety or to weather its storms. But this verse is a bit different: it tells you how *not* to respond.

Many teens who struggle with anxiety and depression are understandably desperate for a way out—so they turn to harmful substances like drugs or alcohol to relieve the anguish. It may work. . .for a while. Intoxication can feel good and even liberating, but this only leads to a reliance that outlasts its purpose. Once a person's anxiety and depression pass (and they will), he's often left with a problem just as bad, if not worse: addiction.

Obviously, there are good reasons to use doctor-prescribed medication to reduce severe levels of stress or depression. But taking matters into your own hands is *never* the way to go. At the bottom of the glass lies not freedom but an even stronger chain to bind your soul.

Today, take the Bible's advice: don't be deceived by the allure of drugs and alcohol.

PRAYER STARTER:

Lord, help me fight my anxiety and depression with tools that honor You, not with self-destructive ones.

BASELESS FEARS

Let your requests be made known to God.
PHILIPPIANS 4:6 ESV

. . . .

One of the best ways to treat anxiety is by simply expressing your fears. A notepad or a listening ear can be the best weapons against fearful or anxious thoughts. Once you get your negative emotions out in the open and express them in a clear, precise way, you often start to realize just how baseless these monstrous feelings are.

Today's verse is a great way to practice this form of therapy. . .only this time, with God as your listener. Be as specific as possible with God when you pray. Don't settle for weak, nebulous prayers that could mean any- thing—tell Him the nitty-gritty details of your fears. If it sounds absurd, don't worry: He's not going to laugh at you. He made your mind, so He already knows all the ways it can turn against you. He understands your torment. . .and He wants nothing more than for you to come to Him for help.

Today, let your requests be made known to God. He's always listening.

PRAYER STARTER:

Father God, thank You for willingly listening to my fears as I express them to You. Teach me to hold nothing back.

BODILY TRAINING

For while bodily training is of some value,
godliness is of value in every way.
1 TIMOTHY 4:8 ESV

While the Bible never addresses the specific benefits of exercise, it does sometimes use the act as a positive metaphor for the Christian walk. And today's verse openly admits that "bodily training" is good for you.

Well, guess what? Modern science has discovered this statement is true in more ways than one. Recent research has shown that exercise—such as a brisk walk outdoors—can drastically decrease your levels of anxiety by channeling all your pent-up adrenaline into something productive. And depression is no different. Some studies, in fact, have proven that a consistent exercise routine is just as effective as medicine in treating chronic sadness.

Clearly, exercise is a gift from God, so we'd be wise to take advantage of it as much as possible. It's just one more tool in our fight to take back our mental health.

PRAYER STARTER:

Thank You, Jesus, for giving us so many natural methods to calm the troubled mind. Help me take advantage of these gifts whenever I need them.

ALL-NATURAL

*Lord, how many are Your works! In wisdom
You have made them all; the earth is full of
Your possessions. There is the sea, great
and broad, in which are swarms without
number, animals both small and great.*
PSALM 104:24–25 NASB

Have you ever noticed your anxiety levels going down
while you were walking outdoors? If so, you're not
imagining things. Scientists have found that the mere
act of being in nature can treat not only anxiety dis-
orders but mild to moderate depression. Why? The
specific biological reasons for this are complex, but
today's scripture suggests the ultimate reason: nature
proves God's glory.

Perhaps God has wired our brains to find a certain
measure of peace in nature so that we can better con-
template His greatness. After all, it's hard to look at a
mighty mountain range or a tiny hummingbird without
thinking of the designer who made them. The world
around us proclaims the name of its maker, and for the
Christian, that's the most relaxing sound of them all.

PRAYER STARTER:

*Thank You, God, for the all-natural stress reliever
that surrounds me. Teach me to better appreciate
Your handiwork by finding rest in its splendor.*

UNSTEADY VS. STEADY

Jesus Christ is the same yesterday, today, and forever.
HEBREWS 13:8 NLT

. . . .

By definition, the anxious brain can't be a stable one. If you struggle with chronic anxiety, every day is a grab bag of stress and fear. What bothered you yesterday may be replaced by a wholly new fear today, and then that fear is replaced by a thought that bothered you three weeks ago. And on the process goes with no relief in sight.

That's why today's verse is so encouraging. It promises that no matter how many tricks your brain plays on you, Jesus is unchanging. Your thoughts, your emotions, and even your attitudes toward God might change from day to day, but He remains the same. One day, you may find peace in His salvation—the next day, you may feel terrified of His perceived anger. But on both days, He has one thought toward you: love. He understands your anxious thoughts and nagging insecurities, so they'll never alter His opinion of you.

Today, find peace in the unchangeability of Jesus Christ!

PRAYER STARTER:

Lord Jesus, my mind is a mess sometimes.
Thank You for being steady in Your love for me,
even when everything about me is unsteady.

SUCH A TIME AS THIS

"Who knows whether you have not attained royalty for such a time as this?"
ESTHER 4:14 NASB

. . . .

If you struggle with depression, you're probably well acquainted with the lies it feeds you daily. *You have no purpose. Everything you do is meaningless. Why not just give up?*

For a healthy mind, these intrusions are the mental equivalent of an internet troll—annoying but easy to ignore. But depression has a way of giving greater weight to these hurtful words. If you feed the troll long enough by ruminating on these thoughts, you'll soon find yourself wondering if maybe they might be true after all.

They're not. Today's verse, spoken by Mordecai to Esther as she prepared to save her people, shows that every choice we make—every moment of our lives—is leading us onward to a higher purpose. Your existence is more than the classes you take, the chores you do, the nights you spend awake, or the frustrations you feel. Your life has a purpose that *far* exceeds the sum of its parts, so giving up is simply out of the question. Even when you can't see it, God has placed you here for such a time as this.

PRAYER STARTER:

Thank You, God, for giving me a purpose that reaches beyond what I see.

IT'S PERSONAL

"I have called you by name, you are mine."
ISAIAH 43:1 ESV

. . . .

We're all personal beings living in an impersonal world. We all desperately need human interaction, but technology is quickly pushing this basic necessity to the fringes. Not long ago, for example, most business transactions were made face-to-face. Then came the telephone, removing the need for travel. Social contact became limited to a human voice. . .which was promptly removed with the advent of email and texting. Eventually, even this spark of personal interaction disappeared—now, the "human" on the other end is most likely a computer.

For teens, this problem extends to social media and online message boards, where creative usernames and humorous profile pics overshadow any real sense of connection. In an age that seems more connected than ever, why is it that nobody seems to know our names? It's a dehumanizing phenomenon that's fueling thoughts of loneliness and isolation. . .and it's only getting worse.

Thankfully, God promises that He still knows your name. You're His—He's chosen you to fulfill a unique and amazing purpose, and He's with you every step of the way.

PRAYER STARTER:

Thank You, Lord, for being a personal
God in an impersonal world.

WORDS ON A SCREEN

When he was reviled, he did not revile in return; when he suffered, he did not threaten, but continued entrusting himself to him who judges justly.
1 PETER 2:23 ESV

. . . .

Just a few years ago, the most common form of bullying among teens was the schoolyard variety: the "strong guy" would push another student or yell insults at him until he gave up his lunch money or apologized for a perceived slight. It was often very public. . .and thus a lot easier to report.

Times have changed. . .but the human heart has not. Cyberbullying is now the dominant form of harassment, and its anonymity often opens teens up to new levels of cruelty. But no matter how often or intense these attacks get, remember that the one thing the bully wants is for you to sink to his level. Don't give him that. Instead, respond with kindness. . .or even better, don't respond at all. Simply report the bully to a trusted adult and open up to your friends and family about the experience.

Don't let hateful words spoken from an insecure heart drag you down—God's love is stronger than any bully, anywhere.

PRAYER STARTER:

Lord, help me to respond to bullying in a way that both stops the process and honors You.

TRAUMA

You keep track of all my sorrows.
You have collected all my tears in your bottle.
You have recorded each one in your book.
PSALM 56:8 NLT

. . . .

Unresolved trauma. These two words form the backbone of many teens' emotional struggles. Dark memories of a past event lurk like demons in the back of the mind, surfacing in nightmares and moments of paralyzing fear. It seems like no one understands—not even your closest friends, family, and counselors.

But God knows. When Jesus came to earth, He was mocked, spat upon, beaten, and subjected to the worst death imaginable. Even after He rose to life again, those memories were there. He vividly recalls His trauma, so He can relate with yours. He understands. He cares.

Today, don't bottle up your emotions. Don't believe the lie that your trauma makes you dirty or unclean. Tell God about the past that haunts your present. Explain your feelings to Him, knowing that He's always listening and relating to your pain. Your trauma may be unresolved. . .but God's love for you is definite.

PRAYER STARTER:

Lord Jesus, I'm holding nothing back.
You know and relate to my trauma, so help me
to share it freely with You. I know You care.

GUILT TRIPS

For the Lord will not reject forever, for if He causes grief, then He will have compassion in proportion to His abundant mercy. For He does not afflict willingly or grieve the sons of mankind.
LAMENTATIONS 3:31–33 NASB

. . . .

God's not big on guilt trips. Sure, if you begin flagrantly disobeying Him, He's going to let you know. After all, a little discipline is sometimes necessary to prevent a world of hurt later on. But if you've confessed your sin and are trying to serve Him, guilt has no place in your life. Whatever you may have done is long gone in God's eyes—it's been erased from existence (Psalm 32:2), and He doesn't even remember it (Hebrews 8:12).

In other words, there's no need to feel guilt over a sin that no longer exists. If you struggle with shame and regret, feel free to seek help and work toward tearing down the thorns that stab at your mind. Such guilt is never from God, so you don't have to treat it like it is.

Today, embrace the freedom that comes with God's forgiveness.

PRAYER STARTER:

Father, I know You've forgotten my mistakes. . .but it's harder for me to do the same. Teach me how to move on before guilt starts taking a toll on my mind and soul.

STEP BY STEP

"Look at the birds. They don't plant or harvest or store food in barns, for your heavenly Father feeds them. And aren't you far more valuable to him than they are?"
MATTHEW 6:26 NLT

. . . .

Do you sometimes feel anxious when you see a huge task ahead of you? Maybe it's writing a research project or taking a complex class or trying your first job or even getting your driver's license. As you set out on this new adventure, all the steps that lie ahead can seem overwhelming. You simply can't imagine how you'll get through everything with your sanity intact.

That outlook fits hand in glove with anxiety. Anxiety often fuels it, and it in turn fuels anxiety. But today's verse offers a way to break the cycle.

Jesus said that no matter how confusing or uncertain the future may seem, we don't have to worry ourselves about it. Just like the birds don't stress over tomorrow, we should learn to take things one step at a time, trusting that God will give us the wisdom for whatever we need to do next.

PRAYER STARTER:

God, help me to approach my long-term goals with a short-term focus. May I take life one day at a time without losing sight of my overarching journey home.

GIVING AND GETTING

"Your giving should be in secret. Then your Father Who sees in secret will reward you."
MATTHEW 6:4 NLV

Out of all the methods you can use to combat anxiety and depression, the act of giving might be the hardest to understand. After all, how can giving away things that make you happy somehow make you even happier? The answer: by shifting the focus off your own problems and toward solving the problems of others.

If you don't have much money, don't worry: *giving* is not just a financial word. You can give up some of your time (volunteering) or resources (sharing), or you could even give someone your undivided attention whenever you feel like walking away. All these things are paths toward generosity. . .and today's verse promises that God will reward you for doing them. This reward may take many forms, but you may find that relief from negative thoughts will be the greatest.

Today, don't let your fight against anxiety and depression morph into an excuse for selfishness—incorporate generosity into your daily routine.

PRAYER STARTER:

Thank You, Jesus, for being generous to me. Help me to show this generosity toward others so that I may find true happiness in the things I give away.

FEAR HAMMER

*"I give them eternal life, and they will never perish,
and no one will snatch them out of my hand."*
JOHN 10:28 ESV

. . . .

Anxiety has a way of taking a person's worst fear—
which, for a Christian, is often the fear of being separated from God—and driving it so deep into the brain
that it feels impossible to remove. With each strike of
the hammer, the brain tells itself that it must adjust to
absorb this new, frightening information. . .when in
reality, it's shattering under the pressure.

Today's verse flips the hammer around, giving you
the tool you need to begin removing this oppression.

God's love for you is so strong that nothing—not
even your deepest fear or regret—can separate you
from Him. You'll never be so dirty or unclean that God
can't clean you up and forgive you. The fevered whis-
perings in your brain—the accusations and guilt and
pain—are just delusions sent either from the misfiring
of the brain or from Satan himself.

You no longer have to comply with these impossible
demands. With God's help, straighten your spine and
start pulling out some nails today!

PRAYER STARTER:

*Thank You, Jesus, for the assuring promise in
today's verse. Help me to use the knowledge of Your
love to pull out the nails of fear and insecurity.*

SUDDEN FALL

If I should say, "My foot has slipped,"
Your faithfulness, Lord, will support me.
PSALM 94:18 NASB

. . . .

Have you ever tried falling asleep, only to be jerked back into awareness by the sudden sense that you're plummeting into an abyss? If so, you probably know how similar this feeling is to the experience of having a panic attack. In both scenarios, you feel as if the ground beneath you has crumbled, sending you free falling through a nightmarish part of your mind you never knew existed. It feels like the very worst you can imagine awaits you at the bottom.

Judging by today's verse, the psalmist experienced these moments of blind terror as well. . .and he relied on God's promises to find his footing.

Over and over again, the Bible tells us that God will never leave us, so anytime you feel like He has, realize that it's your panic talking, not reality. Not only is God holding you steady, He's holding *you*. You don't have to find the ground—you're safe and sound in His hands.

PRAYER STARTER:

Lord God, I thank You for holding me when I feel like I'm falling. When panic threatens to take over, remind me of the power of Your love.

LOOK UP!

But thou, O Lᴏʀᴅ, art a shield for me;
my glory, and the lifter up of mine head.
Pꜱᴀʟᴍ 3:3 ᴋᴊᴠ

. . . .

Some situations in life are so troubling that they cause us to hang our heads in despair, afraid to look ahead for fear of what the future might hold. At least, that's how it begins. Pretty soon, we get comfortable looking down—our own feet seemingly become more interesting to us than anything else.

But, as we all know, staring at our feet is a surefire way to stumble and get lost.

Today's verse promises that if we trust in the Lord, He will lift our heads, giving us the vision we desperately need to get beyond today's pain and into tomorrow's hope. No longer do we have to turn our attention downward or inward; instead, we can look straight ahead. . .even better than that, straight up! Above us is the guide who will guide us home, and the only way we can find true success is by following Him each day.

Let God lift your head with His assurances of a brighter future. . .and then keep walking.

PRAYER STARTER:

Father, I need Your help sometimes to look beyond this present sadness and upward toward Your plan. Lift my head, lest I wander too far from Your will.

VICTORY

*David replied to the Philistine, "You come to me
with sword, spear, and javelin, but I come to you in
the name of the LORD of Heaven's Armies—the God
of the armies of Israel, whom you have defied."*
1 SAMUEL 17:45 NLT

. . . .

Today's verse, spoken by David to Goliath, is one of the
most empowering speeches of the Bible—a brutal take-
down of the enemy's misplaced pride. But notice that it
doesn't come after David's victory. By all appearances,
the boast is premature. Goliath had David outgunned,
a million to one. Who was this shepherd boy to be
making such grandiose threats?

If you struggle with anxiety or depression, you may
feel like David, facing down a giant with nothing but
five pebbles and a sling. After all, how do you wage a
war against your own mind? Is that even possible? The
answer is no. . .not by yourself, that is. The darkness
in your heart is simply too powerful to defeat on your
own. It takes God's help for your stone to hit its mark.

Today, don't struggle against your own fears in
your own power. Ask God to give you the strength to
deliver the killing blow.

PRAYER STARTER:

*God, I'm trusting in Your strength to
wage war against my harmful thoughts.
Help me to obtain the victory today.*

UNQUALIFIED

*Instead, God chose things the world considers
foolish in order to shame those who think
they are wise. And he chose things that are
powerless to shame those who are powerful.*
1 CORINTHIANS 1:27 NLT

• •

Moses, Gideon, and John the Baptist. What do these three guys, each living hundreds of years apart, have in common? That's right: all three, at one point in their lives, experienced extreme levels of doubt and fear. Moses kept telling God he wasn't good enough. Gideon repeatedly sought a sign. And John the Baptist, while in prison, briefly lost his confidence in Jesus.

But there's one other thing these guys have in common: They were all outstanding heroes of the faith, ushering in new eras for God's people. God used them despite (and perhaps even *because of*) their fears and insecurities. He used methods many would call foolish to pave the way for the greatest story ever told: Jesus' death and resurrection.

The next time you think your anxiety disqualifies you from God's service, think again. God loves using people nobody else would have picked!

PRAYER STARTER:

*Lord, please use me despite my anxiety.
Help me to step out on faith and watch
as Your power wipes away my fears.*

FORSAKEN?

My God, my God, why hast thou forsaken me?
PSALM 22:1; MATTHEW 27:46 KJV

. . . .

Today's scripture might be the most gut-wrenching question in the Bible. Not only did the psalmist cry it out during a moment of extreme distress, but Jesus Himself employed it during the darkest time of His life: His crucifixion. That's right: the Son of God Himself felt cut off from His Father.

At the bottom of the well of depression lies a feeling of complete abandonment. It doesn't matter if it isn't true—it *feels* true, and it's the most painful emotion in the world. But even in this dark night of despair, don't lose hope! Remember that the same psalmist who cried out these words also found the strength, just a few verses later, to proclaim, "My praise shall be of thee in the great congregation" (22:25 KJV), and that Jesus' cry of anguish was rectified when He rose from the dead.

God never leaves His children, even when we feel like He has. All it takes is a little more endurance before even the darkest of nights gives way to light of day.

PRAYER STARTER:

*Lord, when I feel cut off from Your presence,
I know in my heart that You're still here.
That's what You've promised, so that's what I believe.*

UNBREAKABLE COVENANT

"For the mountains may be removed and the hills may shake, but My favor will not be removed from you, nor will My covenant of peace be shaken," says the Lord who has compassion on you.
ISAIAH 54:10 NASB

. . . .

The world is ending. Everything's falling apart. I'm just one step away from calamity. It's all over. I'm going to die.

If you've ever had a severe panic attack, these thoughts might seem disturbingly familiar. Once the panic reaches this point, you realize, no amount of rationality can refute these surging emotions: they become as real as if these events were playing out before your eyes. That's why today's verse, whose imagery shockingly resembles that of a panic attack, can be a comfort to anyone who suffers from chronic anxiety.

Even in the height of your fear—at the moment you run out of breath and your tears break loose—God's covenant with you stands strong. *Nothing*, not even the impending doom that seems so real at the time, can separate you from His grace and love. So whenever you feel the panic start to surge, let today's verse be the raft that helps you ride out this awful wave.

PRAYER STARTER:

Lord, thank You for this reassuring confirmation of Your unbreakable covenant. Remind me of its truth when my emotions run wild.

A SINGLE ISLAND

"My sheep hear my voice, and I know them, and they follow me."
JOHN 10:27 ESV

. . . .

In a scene from the 2013 movie *Man of Steel*, a young Superman is having a mental breakdown at school. The true extent of his powers is just beginning to manifest, and he's at first unable to cope with their intensity. His world becomes chaos, crowded with X-ray images of the people around him and the mocking whispers of his classmates. Overwhelmed by this sensory overload, he cries out to his mom, who happens to be standing nearby, "The world's too big!" She responds, "Then make it small. Just focus on my voice. Pretend it's an island, out in the ocean."

As Christians, we live in a big world that's filled with dissonant, incoherent voices, all trying to win our devotion. Attempting to listen to all of them at once will lead to unbearable pain. . .just like it did for young Clark Kent. That's why Jesus' words in today's verse are so refreshing: they tell us that His voice is the only voice that matters—a single island in a sea of confusion.

Whose voice are you listening to today?

PRAYER STARTER:

Lord, help me to tune out the world's distressing static and focus solely on Your truth.

TOO GREAT

*O Lord, my heart is not lifted up; my eyes are
not raised too high; I do not occupy myself with
things too great and too marvelous for me.*

PSALM 131:1 ESV

. . . .

Some people may say this verse discourages learning
and stretching our brains. After all, the entirety of sci-
entific progress is built on trying to understand things
we haven't figured out yet, so why would the psalmist
say that's a bad thing?

But that's not what this verse means. For a better
application, think of the last time you lay awake at night
wondering about the future. . .about the mysteries
of God. . .about the nature of existence. Chances are
(especially if you already struggle with anxiety), these
thoughts sparked a deep unease that lingered through
the night. Why? Because the very nature of these
questions ensures we'll never know the answers to
them. They're simply too great for us. . .and that's okay.

Because God knows everything, we don't have to.
When we feel overwhelmed by the seemingly infinite
chasm in our understanding, we can rest assured,
knowing God's love for us is infinite as well.

PRAYER STARTER:

*God, thank You for relieving my burden by taking
care of the things that are past my understanding.
Help me to find peace in not knowing.*

CRUSHED TO SMITHEREENS

*The God of peace will soon crush
Satan under your feet.*
ROMANS 16:20 NASB

Evil and despair and hopelessness are running ram-pant in our world. Satan loves every minute of it. All he has to do is give this culture a little nudge, and it seems humanity's self-destructive tendencies do the rest for him.

Given that the world is rapidly turning into a cesspool of sin and suffering, shouldn't Christians be terrified? Today's verse gives us the answer: *nope.* Satan may have a lot of power now, and his deceptions may appear more convincing than ever—but for the Christian teen whose hope lies in God's Word, the devil's perceived victory is little more than a last-second grab at power before he's defeated once and for all. And rest assured: defeat is the *only* outcome for Satan. God's power will soon crush the forces of evil like soda cans under the wheels of a semi. . .and He'll use His children to do it.

Today, reject the lies of anxiety in favor of the truth of God's power.

PRAYER STARTER:

*Thank You for promising victory for
Your children, God. Help me to live in
the light of this triumphant future.*

FOUNDATIONAL PEACE

For he himself is our peace, who has made us both one and has broken down in his flesh the dividing wall of hostility.
EPHESIANS 2:14 ESV

. . . .

Know God, know peace. No God, no peace.

Maybe you've seen this slogan on church signs or religious tracts. But have you ever stopped to consider how revolutionary this statement is? After all, the most valuable commodity in the universe right now is peace. . .and it seems nobody is able to find it. But if this saying is true, that means the answer was right in front of us all along.

Well, today's verse takes this a step further. It says God and peace aren't just related through cause and effect—they're one and the same. God *is* peace. If you know God, true peace is a given. Of course, this doesn't mean you'll never feel afraid; rather, it means you'll always have a concrete foundation that lies below the emotional sludge that occasionally fills your mind. Even in the midst of uncertainty, your feet can rest on the promises of Peace Himself.

PRAYER STARTER:

Lord God, thank You for being my peace. As long as You're here, my anxiety will never remove the bedrock of purpose that undergirds my life.

IT'S A METAPHOR

*The people who walk in darkness will
see a great light; those who live in a dark
land, the light will shine on them.*

ISAIAH 9:2 NASB

. . . .

If you haven't noticed by now, God loves using light/
dark metaphors to describe His relationship with the
world. The Lord who made the sun and moon and
causes the earth to turn on its axis is the same Lord
who regularly employs His own creation as illustrations
to help us better understand Him.

In other words, the God who fashioned the night,
giving it a purpose and determining just how long it
should last, is the same God who paints the sunrise
each morning, reminding us that all darkness eventually
comes to an end. So whenever you're going through
a dark period, know that this isn't some unexpected
development or a threat to God's sovereignty. Rather,
it's nothing but another night—a hard but limited time
of uncertainty that's expressly designed to fortify
your faith.

Even when the skies are black, you can rest in the
assurance that sunrise is coming.

PRAYER STARTER:

*Lord, give me the strength to make it through this
night. I can't wait to see Your splendid sunrise.*

HUMBLE YOURSELF

*So humble yourselves under the mighty
power of God, and at the right time he will
lift you up in honor. Give all your worries and
cares to God, for he cares about you.*
1 PETER 5:6–7 NLT

. . . .

Oddly enough, many of our deepest fears stem from
an inappropriate attitude toward our own abilities.
We think we *should* be able to tackle this problem all
by ourselves, so when we find we can't, it sends our
mind into a tailspin. We start fixating on irrational
ideas, foolishly believing we can somehow solve the
unsolvable if only we worry a little bit more.

That's why today's scripture tells us to humble
ourselves before God. Once we have the right idea
about who God is, we're left with no reason to worry.
We know full well that we can't solve this huge problem, but we also know we don't have to, for God has
already solved it for us. Suddenly, the cycle of endless
worry and fear grows quaint and unnecessary. We find
ourselves free to admit our weaknesses. . .and free to
lean on God.

PRAYER STARTER:

*Lord, sometimes I'm a nervous mess, but I
know I don't have to be. Please give me a
proper understanding of Your power so that
I can rely on You to conquer my fears.*

NEVER AGAIN

And God shall wipe away all tears from their eyes; and there shall be no more death, neither sorrow, nor crying, neither shall there be any more pain: for the former things are passed away.
REVELATION 21:4 KJV

Doesn't this verse sound amazing? In a life filled with uncertainties, hurt, sorrow, and loss, doesn't the prospect of a future life with none of these things sound too good to be true?

Well, it *is* true! God has designed every aspect of this life—our joys as well as our tears—to lead us on to our eternal home with Him. Each moment of happiness reminds us of the perfect joy that awaits. . . and each moment of fear and suffering reminds us of the day when all these things will be wiped away. Even through the tears of depression and the fires of panic, you can look to today's verse for a hope that surpasses understanding.

Not only is God with you now, He's in it for the long haul. And at the end of your life, He'll still be there, arms open wide, eager to wipe away your tears once and for all.

PRAYER STARTER:

Thank You, heavenly Father, for such a relieving promise. The truth of heaven makes the lies of fear and sadness easier to ignore.

SCRIPTURE INDEX